Florida DMV Exam Prep

Ace Your Exam on the First Try with Practice Questions, In-Depth Explanations, Realistic Exam-Style Quizzes, and an Online Simulator for Quick, Unlimited Practice

Ryan Foster

Table of Contents

Introduction

Welcome to the ultimate guide for obtaining your driver's license in the state of Florida. This book has been created to provide you with all the essential information needed to navigate the process of getting your license, whether you're a young person obtaining your license for the first time, relocating from another state, or simply renewing your existing license.

Obtaining a driver's license is a crucial step towards personal independence and mobility. Florida, with its scenic roads, vibrant cities, and expansive highways, offers a wide range of driving experiences. However, to explore all that Florida has to offer safely and legally, it's essential to understand and adhere to the state's traffic laws and regulations.

This book will guide you step by step through each phase of the process, from preparing the necessary documents to passing the driving exam. We will also cover Florida-specific laws and rules, which may differ from those in other states, and provide you with study strategies and techniques for managing exam stress.

In addition to offering practical information, this guide includes quizzes and practice exams that will help you test your knowledge and prepare thoroughly for the real exam. Each section of the book is designed to be easy to follow and packed with useful details, so you can approach the process with confidence.

Whether you're a new driver or an experienced one needing to renew your license, this book is here to support you every step of the way. Get ready to get behind the wheel safely and confidently, and to explore everything Florida has to offer.

Basic Requirements

Required Documents

To obtain a driver's license in Florida, it is essential to present a series of documents that verify your identity, residency, and legal status in the United States. The Florida Department of Highway Safety and Motor Vehicles (FLHSMV) requires every applicant to provide the following documents:

- **Proof of Identity:** A valid and recognized document to verify your identity. This can include a government-issued birth certificate, a valid U.S. passport, or a Permanent Resident Card (Green Card). If the name on the document differs from your current name due to marriage, divorce, or other legal reasons, you will need to provide additional documents that confirm the name change.

- **Proof of Social Security Number:** You must present a document that shows your Social Security number. This can be your Social Security card, a tax return, or any other official government-issued document.

- **Proof of Florida Residency:** To prove your residency, you must present at least two recent documents that show your name and current address. These can include a utility bill, a lease agreement, a bank statement, or a government document. If you do not have documents in your name, such as when living with a family member, you may need to provide an affidavit from your host along with their residency documents.

- **Proof of Legal Status in the United States:** If you are not a U.S. citizen, you must provide documents that verify your legal status, such as a Green Card, a work visa, or other immigration documents issued by the government.

Each document must be original or a certified copy. Expired documents, uncertified photocopies, or digital copies will not be accepted. Proper and thorough preparation of your documents is essential to avoid delays in the process of obtaining your license.

Preparing for the Application

Before attending your appointment at the DMV, it's important to prepare and organize all the necessary documents. Thorough preparation will help you avoid potential issues or delays during your application.

1. **Gather the Documents:** Ensure you have all the required documents, as mentioned in the previous subsection. Check that they are up to date and valid. If you need a specific document that you don't have, such as a birth certificate, request it well in advance.

2. **Organize the Documents:** Keep your documents in a logical and easily accessible order. Use a folder to keep all necessary documents together. This will save you time and reduce stress during your DMV appointment.

3. **Verify the Requirements:** Before you go, check the FLHSMV website to ensure that the requirements haven't changed and that there are no recent updates. Regulations can vary, so it's important to stay informed about any changes.

4. **Schedule Your Appointment:** Book your appointment at the DMV in advance. Many DMV offices offer online booking options to help you avoid long waits. Choose a time that allows you to arrive calmly and with everything you need.

5. **Prepare Mentally:** A DMV appointment can be stressful, especially if it's your first time going through this process. Take the time to review the information and make sure you are well-prepared. Bring a copy of your document checklist with you so you can do a final review before your appointment.

By following these steps, you can ensure that your application process goes smoothly and minimize the risk of needing to return to the DMV to correct any errors or omissions.

Verification Process

The document verification process is a crucial part of obtaining a driver's license in Florida. During this process, DMV staff will carefully review each document to ensure it meets state and federal requirements.

1. **Identity Verification:** The first step is to confirm your identity. The primary document you provide, such as a passport or birth certificate, will be thoroughly examined. It's important that the document is authentic and valid. If there are discrepancies in names or personal information, you will need to provide additional documents to clarify the situation.

2. **Residency Verification:** DMV staff will verify the documents that prove your residency in Florida. You will need to provide at least two documents that show your name and current address. These documents must be recent and not expired. In some cases, the DMV may require additional proof if the documents presented are not deemed sufficient.

3. **Social Security Number Verification:** Your Social Security number will be cross-referenced with data provided by the Social Security Administration (SSA). Ensure that the name on your Social Security document matches exactly with the name on your other documents. Discrepancies could cause delays or require further verification.

4. **Legal Status Verification:** For non-U.S. citizens, verifying legal status is a critical step. The DMV will work with the Department of Homeland Security (DHS) to confirm that your legal status allows you to obtain a driver's license. It's important to present all necessary documents and ensure they are current and valid.

5. **Vision Test and Other Checks:** During the verification process, you may also be required to undergo a vision test and other basic checks. The vision test is mandatory and must be passed before you can proceed with obtaining your driver's license. Be sure to bring your glasses or contact lenses if needed.

The verification process can take some time, so it's important to be patient and cooperative. Once all your documents have been verified and approved, you can proceed with the next steps to obtain your driver's license in Florida.

The Learner's Permit

What is a Learner's Permit?

A learner's permit, also known as a "learner's license," is a document issued by the state of Florida that allows new drivers to legally begin driving under certain conditions. This permit represents the first crucial step for anyone seeking to obtain a full driver's license and offers the opportunity to gain practical driving experience in a controlled environment.

Definition and Purpose of the Permit for New Drivers

The learner's permit is primarily intended for young drivers, typically between the ages of 15 and 17, although it is available to anyone who has never held a driver's license, regardless of age. This permit authorizes the holder to drive a vehicle, but only when accompanied by a qualified adult driver, usually a parent or guardian, who is at least 21 years old and holds a valid driver's license.

The utility of the learner's permit lies in its educational purpose. It allows new drivers to accumulate practical road experience in various traffic and weather conditions under the supervision of an experienced adult. This learning period is crucial for developing driving skills, understanding road rules, and building the confidence necessary to drive safely.

In Florida, holders of a learner's permit are subject to specific restrictions designed to ensure their safety and that of other road users. For example, during the first three months after obtaining the permit, drivers are not allowed to drive at night; after that, they may drive only until 10:00 PM. These restrictions help reduce the risks associated with driving in challenging conditions, such as nighttime driving, which can be particularly difficult for new drivers.

In addition to providing practical experience, the learner's permit is also a prerequisite for obtaining a full driver's license. In Florida, young drivers must hold the learner's permit for at least 12 months and accumulate at least 50 hours of supervised driving (including at least 10 hours of nighttime driving) before they can take the driving test for a full license. This learning and practice period is designed to ensure that new drivers are adequately prepared to face the challenges of independent driving.

In summary, the learner's permit is an essential and mandatory stage for all new drivers in Florida. It not only provides the opportunity to learn to drive in a safe environment but also establishes a solid foundation of knowledge and skills necessary to become a responsible and safe driver.

How to Obtain the Permit

Obtaining a learner's permit in Florida involves completing a series of steps that ensure the applicant is ready to begin the process of learning to drive. Here are the main steps that must be followed:

Steps to Apply for the Learner's Permit

1. **Complete the Traffic Law and Substance Abuse Education (TLSAE) Course:**

   o The first step to obtaining a learner's permit in Florida is to complete the TLSAE (Traffic Law and Substance Abuse Education) course. This course is mandatory and must be completed by all new drivers, regardless of age. The course covers essential topics such as Florida traffic laws, substance abuse and its effects on driving ability, and other critical information for road safety.

   o The TLSAE course is available online and through institutions approved by the Florida Department of Highway Safety and Motor Vehicles (FLHSMV). Once you complete the course, you will receive a certificate that you must present to the DMV as part of your learner's permit application.

2. **Prepare the Required Documents:**

   o As discussed in Chapter 1, you need to gather and prepare all the required documents to verify your identity, residency, and legal status. This includes proof of identity, proof of Social Security number, and proof of Florida residency. Ensure that all documents are in order and ready to be presented.

3. **Pass the Knowledge Exam:**

   - Before obtaining the learner's permit, you must pass a written knowledge exam that tests your understanding of Florida traffic laws, road signs, and safe driving practices. The exam covers a variety of topics, including speed limits, right-of-way rules, parking regulations, and more.

   - The knowledge exam can be taken at a DMV office or online through approved providers. It is advisable to study using the Florida Driver's Handbook, which contains all the necessary information to prepare for the exam.

4. **Schedule a DMV Appointment:**

   - After completing the TLSAE course and passing the knowledge exam, the next step is to schedule an appointment at a DMV office to submit your learner's permit application. In Florida, many DMV offices require an appointment, which can be booked online through the FLHSMV website.

5. **Attend the Appointment with the Required Documents:**

   - On the day of your appointment, you must present yourself at the DMV with all the required documents, including the TLSAE course completion certificate, the knowledge exam passing certificate, and documents verifying your identity, residency, and Social Security number. During the appointment, DMV staff will verify your documents and conduct a vision test to ensure you meet the necessary vision requirements for driving.

6. **Receive the Learner's Permit:**

   - Once all your documents have been verified and you have passed the vision test, you will be issued a learner's permit. With this permit, you are authorized to begin driving under the supervision of a qualified adult driver, as discussed in the previous subsection.

7. **Begin the Learning Period:**

   - After obtaining the permit, you can begin your learning period. It is important to use this time to gain driving experience in various conditions and environments, always adhering to the restrictions imposed by the permit. Remember that the permit only allows for supervised driving and does not authorize you to drive alone until you obtain a full driver's license.

By carefully following these steps, you will be able to obtain your learner's permit and start your journey toward getting a driver's license in Florida. Each phase of the process is designed to ensure that you are adequately prepared to become a safe and responsible driver.

Requirements for the Permit

Obtaining a learner's permit in Florida is not just about completing the administrative process; it's crucial to meet a set of specific requirements that demonstrate your eligibility and readiness to begin driving. These requirements are designed to ensure that all new drivers have the necessary skills and preparation to drive safely.

Eligibility Criteria and Specific Requirements for Obtaining the Permit

1. **Age Requirements:**

    o   In Florida, you can apply for a learner's permit starting at the age of 15. However, there are specific restrictions for young drivers, such as a prohibition on driving during nighttime hours within the first three months after the permit is issued.

2. **Completion of the TLSAE Course:**

    o   As mentioned in the previous subsection, completing the TLSAE course is mandatory for all learner's permit applicants. This course must be completed before you can take the knowledge exam and apply for the permit.

3. **Passing the Knowledge Exam:**

    o   All applicants must pass the knowledge exam to demonstrate an adequate understanding of traffic laws, road signs, and safe driving practices. This exam is a fundamental part of the permit process and must be successfully completed before the permit can be issued.

4. **Vision Requirements:**

    o   Applicants must meet the vision requirements set by the DMV. This includes the ability to see clearly at various distances and having good peripheral vision. If you wear glasses or contact lenses, make sure to bring them with you when taking the vision test.

5. **Proper Documentation:**
   - You must present all required documents, such as proof of identity, residency, and Social Security number. Without these documents, the learner's permit cannot be issued.

6. **Payment of Fees:**
   - Finally, obtaining the learner's permit requires the payment of an administrative fee. The cost may vary, so it's advisable to check the exact amount with the DMV or on the FLHSMV website.

Learner's Permit Restrictions

Once obtained, the learner's permit comes with a set of restrictions designed to ensure that new drivers gain experience safely. These restrictions include:

- **Supervised Driving:** The permit holder may only drive when accompanied by an adult who is at least 21 years old, holds a valid driver's license, and is seated next to the driver. This requirement is essential to ensure that the new driver receives real-time instructions and feedback while learning to drive.

- **Time Restrictions:** During the first three months after the permit is issued, the driver is not allowed to drive after sunset. After this period, driving is permitted only until 10:00 PM. These restrictions are intended to prevent new drivers from facing challenging driving conditions, such as nighttime driving, before they have gained sufficient experience.

- **No Solo Driving:** The learner's permit does not allow for unsupervised driving. This is one of the most important rules, as driving without supervision during the learning period is a serious violation that can result in severe penalties, including the suspension of the permit.

- **Passenger Limitations:** In some cases, there may be restrictions on the number of passengers the new driver can carry. This is particularly true for young drivers, to avoid distractions that could increase the risk of accidents.

Duration and Validity of the Learner's Permit

The learner's permit in Florida is valid for 12 months, during which the holder must accumulate at least 50 hours of supervised driving, including at least 10 hours of nighttime driving. If all conditions and requirements are met, the permit holder can then apply to take the driving test to obtain a full license.

Failure to comply with the learner's permit restrictions could result in the extension of the learning period or the suspension of the permit. Therefore, it is essential to follow all the rules and use this time to gain driving experience and confidence.

Application Procedure

Preparing for Your DMV Appointment

Obtaining a learner's permit or driver's license in Florida requires a well-planned and organized process, culminating in an appointment at the Department of Highway Safety and Motor Vehicles (DMV). Preparing for this appointment is crucial to ensure that everything goes smoothly and that your application is approved on the first attempt.

How to Book and Prepare for the Appointment

1. **Book the Appointment:**

   o Booking your DMV appointment is the first essential step. In Florida, it is highly recommended to schedule an appointment online through the FLHSMV website. This allows you to avoid long waits and choose a time that best fits your schedule. Some DMV offices may accept walk-ins, but booking in advance ensures that you are served promptly.

   o When booking your appointment, you will be asked to select the type of service you need, such as "Obtaining a Learner's Permit" or "Renewing a License." Be sure to select the correct option to avoid any issues on the day of your appointment.

2. **Review Requirements and Documents:**

   o Once your appointment is booked, it's essential to review the requirements and necessary documents. As discussed in Chapter 1, you'll need to bring several documents that prove your identity, residency, and legal status. Additionally, ensure you have your TLSAE course completion certificate (if applicable) and your knowledge exam results.

   o Carefully check that all documents are up to date and valid. Photocopies or expired documents will not be accepted, which could delay the process and require you to schedule a new appointment.

3. **Mental and Practical Preparation:**

   ○ In addition to preparing your documents, it's important to mentally prepare for the appointment. The DMV can be a stressful place, especially if you're unsure of what to expect. Take the time to review the process and understand exactly what will happen during the appointment.

   ○ If you're taking the knowledge exam or driving test during the appointment, make sure you're well-prepared. Review study materials, such as the Florida Driver's Handbook, and practice exam questions if possible. Adequate preparation will help you feel more confident and reduce stress.

4. **Logistical Considerations:**

   ○ Before your appointment, verify the location of the DMV office and plan your trip. Consider traffic, parking, and the time needed to arrive calmly. Arriving early will give you time to relax and prepare without rushing.

   ○ Bring everything you need, including documents, any study materials, glasses or contact lenses (if required for the vision test), and a pen. Being well-organized will help you avoid issues during the appointment.

Adequate preparation for your DMV appointment is the best way to ensure that the application process goes smoothly. Good preparation allows you to approach the appointment with confidence and increases your chances of success.

Documents to Present

Bringing the correct documents to the DMV is essential for successfully completing your application for a learner's permit or driver's license in Florida. Missing a necessary document can delay the entire process, requiring you to schedule a new appointment and extending the time needed to obtain your license.

Which Documents to Bring to the DMV

1. **Proof of Identity:**

   o The first required document is proof of identity. This can include a government-issued birth certificate, a valid U.S. passport, or a Permanent Resident Card (Green Card). If the name on your identity document differs from your current name (e.g., due to marriage or a legal name change), you will also need to present documentation that proves the change, such as a marriage certificate or a name change decree.

2. **Proof of Social Security Number:**

   o You must bring a document that shows your Social Security number. This can be your Social Security card, a W-2 form, a 1099 form, or a tax return that lists your Social Security number. Ensure that the name on your Social Security document matches exactly with the name on your other documents.

3. **Proof of Florida Residency:**

   o You will need to provide two documents that prove your residency in Florida. These can include a recent utility bill, a lease agreement, a bank statement, or an official government document that shows your name and current address. If you don't have documents in your name (e.g., if you live with a family member), you may need to present an affidavit from your host along with their residency documents.

4. **TLSAE Course Completion Certificate:**

   o If you are applying for a learner's permit, you must present the certificate of completion for the Traffic Law and Substance Abuse Education (TLSAE) course. This certificate can be obtained online or from an FLHSMV-approved provider. The TLSAE course is mandatory for all new drivers and must be completed before applying for the permit.

5. **Knowledge Exam Results:**

   o If you have already taken and passed the knowledge exam, you will need to bring your exam results with you. This is particularly important if the exam was taken online or through an external provider. If you haven't taken the exam yet, it will be scheduled during your DMV appointment.

6. **Proof of Legal Status in the United States:**

   - If you are not a U.S. citizen, you must present documents that prove your legal status in the United States, such as a Green Card, a valid work visa, or other government-issued immigration documents.

7. **Payment of Fees:**

   - Ensure that you bring an accepted form of payment to cover the administrative fees associated with your application. The fees may vary depending on the type of permit or license you are applying for, so check the exact amount and accepted payment methods (cash, credit card, check, etc.) in advance.

Bringing all the required documents and ensuring they are in order is crucial to making sure the application process goes smoothly. If documents are missing or there are discrepancies, your appointment may be rescheduled, extending the time needed to obtain your learner's permit or driver's license.

Steps During the Appointment

Once you arrive at your DMV appointment with all the necessary documents, it's important to know what to expect during the process. This will help you feel more prepared and reduce any anxiety associated with the experience.

What Happens During the DMV Appointment

1. **Check-In and Registration:**

   o When you arrive at the DMV, the first thing you will need to do is check in. Often, there will be a reception desk or an electronic kiosk where you can enter your information and indicate the purpose of your visit. If you have scheduled an appointment, the system will assign you a waiting number and direct you to where you should wait for your turn.

   o During registration, make sure you have your appointment confirmation (if you booked online) and key documents like your ID card handy.

2. **Document Verification:**

   o Once called, a DMV representative will review your documents. This is a critical step, as the representative will carefully check that all your documents are correct and in order. This includes verifying your identity, Social Security number, residency, and legal status in the United States.

   o If any document is not in compliance, you may need to provide additional documentation or schedule a new appointment. This is why thorough document preparation, as discussed in Chapter 1, is essential.

3. **Vision Test:**

   o If you are applying for a learner's permit or a new driver's license, you will need to undergo a vision test. This test is crucial to ensure that you have the necessary visual acuity to drive safely.

   o The vision test is conducted directly at the DMV and involves reading a series of letters or numbers from a certain distance, similar to an eye exam. If you wear glasses or contact lenses, be sure to wear them during the test.

4. **Knowledge Exam (if not already completed):**

   o If you haven't yet taken the knowledge exam online, this will be the time to do so. The exam covers traffic laws, road signs, and safe driving practices, as discussed in detail in Chapter 2.

   o The exam is usually made up of multiple-choice questions and can be completed on a computer. If you pass the exam, the results will be available immediately, and you can proceed to the next step of the application process.

5. **Issuance of the Learner's Permit or Driver's License:**

   o Once all necessary checks and exams are completed, the DMV will proceed with issuing your learner's permit or driver's license. You will be asked to sign the document and have your photo taken, which will appear on your license.

   o You will receive a temporary copy of your permit or license, which will be valid until you receive the permanent version by mail. This temporary document authorizes you to begin driving immediately, according to the applicable restrictions.

6. **Payment of Fees:**

   o Before concluding the appointment, you will need to pay the administrative fees. As discussed in Chapter 1, it's important to bring an accepted form of payment to the DMV. Fees vary depending on the type of permit or license you are applying for, so be prepared.

7. **Confirmation and Receipt of Document:**

   o At the end of the process, you will be provided with a confirmation of your payment and information, along with an approximate date when you will receive your permanent driver's license or learner's permit.

   o Be sure to check all the information on your temporary license to ensure it is correct. If you notice any errors, report them to the DMV staff immediately.

Being prepared for what will happen during your appointment will help you feel more confident and reduce stress. Knowing what to expect can make the difference between a smooth experience and one that might require additional visits and time.

Knowledge and Driving Exams

Obtaining a driver's license in Florida requires passing several exams designed to ensure that new drivers are adequately prepared to drive safely on public roads. These exams include the knowledge test and, subsequently, the practical driving test. In this subsection, we will examine both in detail.

Overview of the Exams to Be Taken

1. **Knowledge Exam:**

   o The knowledge exam is a written test that assesses your understanding of traffic laws, road signs, and safe driving practices. As discussed in Chapter 2, this exam is a prerequisite for obtaining a learner's permit and must be passed before you can proceed to the practical driving test.

   o The test consists of a series of multiple-choice questions, generally based on the Florida Driver's Handbook. Topics covered include speed limits, right-of-way rules, parking regulations, and penalties for traffic violations, among others.

   o The knowledge exam can be taken online through authorized providers or directly at a DMV office. If the exam is taken online, the results will be automatically transmitted to the DMV, simplifying the process of issuing the permit.

2. **Practical Driving Exam:**

   o After passing the knowledge exam and obtaining the learner's permit, the next step is the practical driving exam, which evaluates your actual driving skills. This exam is typically required after you have accumulated sufficient supervised driving experience, as discussed in previous chapters.

   o The practical driving exam is conducted by a licensed examiner at a DMV testing center. During the exam, you will be asked to demonstrate a series of maneuvers, such as parallel parking, entering and exiting a roadway, making U-turns, correctly using turn signals, and managing intersections and traffic lights.

o   The evaluation is based on your ability to perform these maneuvers safely and correctly while following traffic rules. The examiner will also assess your awareness of other vehicles and pedestrians, as well as your ability to maintain control of the vehicle in various situations.

3. **Preparing for the Exams:**

   o   Preparation is key to passing both exams. For the knowledge exam, it is advisable to study the Florida Driver's Handbook, take practice quizzes, and review frequently asked questions. Many online resources offer exam simulations that can help you become familiar with the question format.

   o   For the practical driving exam, actual driving experience is crucial. Driving in different conditions (day, night, rain) and in various environments (urban, rural) will help you feel more comfortable during the exam. Taking driving lessons with a certified instructor can also be very helpful in receiving feedback and improving your skills.

4. **What Happens After the Exams:**

   o   If you pass the knowledge exam, you will receive your learner's permit, allowing you to begin supervised driving. After accumulating the required experience, you can schedule the practical driving exam.

   o   Once you pass the practical driving exam, you will obtain your full driver's license. If you do not pass one of the exams, you can retake it, but you may need to wait a certain period and, in some cases, pay a retesting fee.

The Knowledge Exam

Overview of the Exam

The knowledge exam, also known as the written test, is a crucial step in obtaining a learner's permit or driver's license in Florida. This exam is designed to assess your understanding of traffic laws, road signs, and safe driving practices. Passing this exam is a mandatory requirement before you can proceed to the practical driving test.

Structure and Content of the Knowledge Exam

The knowledge exam in Florida consists of a series of multiple-choice questions covering a wide range of driving-related topics. Typically, the exam includes 50 questions, and to pass, you must answer at least 80% of the questions correctly (which means 40 correct answers out of 50). Here is an overview of the main topics that will be covered:

1. **Traffic Laws:**

   o This section covers the fundamental rules of the road, such as speed limits, right-of-way rules, seat belt usage, and specific regulations for certain traffic situations, like railroad crossings and intersections.

   o You will also be tested on Florida-specific laws, such as right-of-way regulations at roundabouts, the requirement to stop for pedestrians in crosswalks, and restrictions on electronic devices while driving.

2. **Road Signs:**

   o Questions in this section will ask you to identify and interpret various road signs you might encounter on Florida roads. This includes regulatory signs, warning signs, informational signs, and work zone signs.

   o You'll need to understand what different colors and shapes of signs indicate, as well as the importance of the symbols they represent.

3. **Safe Driving Practices:**

   o This section assesses your understanding of defensive driving techniques and safety practices that can prevent accidents. Questions might cover the importance of maintaining a safe following distance, how to handle emergency situations, and how to adjust your driving in adverse weather conditions.

   o You will also be tested on how to deal with aggressive or distracted drivers and how to navigate through heavy traffic.

4. **Emergency Procedures:**

   o Some questions may focus on what to do in case of a roadside emergency, how to respond in the event of an accident, and what steps to take if your vehicle breaks down in a dangerous location.

   o You'll need to know the procedures for calling for help, how to use your vehicle's emergency signals, and what precautions to take in hazardous situations.

The knowledge exam can be taken at a DMV office or online through authorized FLHSMV providers. If you choose to take the exam online, be sure to select an accredited provider to ensure that the results are accepted by the DMV.

4.2 Sample Questions and Answers

To prepare effectively for the knowledge exam, it's helpful to review some sample questions and answers. These examples reflect the type of content you may encounter on the test and will help you become familiar with the question format.

Examples of Questions That May Appear on the Exam

1. **Question:** What is the speed limit in a residential area in Florida unless otherwise posted?

   o A) 25 mph

   o B) 35 mph

   o C) 45 mph

   o D) 55 mph

   o **Correct Answer:** A) 25 mph

2. **Question:** What should you do when you see a road sign with the word "STOP"?

   o A) Slow down and check for traffic, then proceed without stopping

   o B) Come to a complete stop and check traffic in all directions before proceeding

   o C) Stop only if there are oncoming vehicles

   o D) Stop only if there are pedestrians crossing

   o **Correct Answer:** B) Come to a complete stop and check traffic in all directions before proceeding

3. **Question:** In which of the following situations is it illegal to pass another vehicle?

   o A) In a zone with double solid center lines

   o B) On a one-way street

   o C) When a vehicle is approaching from behind

   o D) When driving less than 10 mph below the speed limit

   o **Correct Answer:** A) In a zone with double solid center lines

4. **Question:** What is the minimum following distance you must maintain from a vehicle you are following?

   - A) Two seconds
   - B) Three seconds
   - C) Five seconds
   - D) Ten seconds
   - **Correct Answer:** B) Three seconds

5. **Question:** What is the correct procedure for making a right turn at an intersection with a green traffic light?

   - A) Turn immediately without stopping
   - B) Slow down, check for pedestrian traffic, and make the turn
   - C) Come to a complete stop, check for traffic, then make the turn
   - D) Turn only if there are no other vehicles approaching
   - **Correct Answer:** B) Slow down, check for pedestrian traffic, and make the turn

These examples give you an idea of what to expect during the exam. It's important not only to memorize the answers but also to understand the reasoning behind each correct answer, as this will help you make better decisions in real-life driving situations.

Study Strategies

Effectively preparing for the knowledge exam requires a combination of dedicated study, practice, and time management. Here are some study strategies that can help maximize your chances of success.

Tips for Effective Preparation

1. **Study the Florida Driver's Handbook:**

   o The Florida Driver's Handbook is your primary source of information for the knowledge exam. It covers all the traffic laws, road signs, and safe driving practices that will be tested in the exam. Spend time carefully reading each section of the handbook, taking notes on key points.

   o Focus on chapters that cover more complex topics or those you are less familiar with. For example, Florida-specific laws or less common road signs.

2. **Utilize Online Resources:**

   o In addition to the handbook, there are many online resources that offer practice quizzes and exam simulations. These tools are useful for testing your knowledge and familiarizing yourself with the question format. Many websites offer multiple-choice questions similar to those you will find on the official exam.

   o Some mobile apps are designed to help you study interactively, allowing you to practice wherever you are. These apps can be particularly useful for reviewing when you only have a few minutes to spare.

3. **Create a Study Plan:**

   o Plan your study schedule well in advance of the exam date. A good study plan breaks down the material into manageable sections, allowing you to focus on one topic at a time. For example, you might dedicate one day to studying traffic laws, another to road signs, and so on.

   o Regularly review the material you've studied to reinforce your memory. Use techniques like flashcards or concept maps to help you memorize important information.

4. **Take Practice Exams:**

   o Taking practice exams is one of the best strategies for preparing. Practice tests allow you to test your knowledge in an environment similar to the real exam. They will help you identify areas where you are strong and those that need further study.

   o Try to take as many practice exams as possible and carefully review any questions you answered incorrectly. Understanding your mistakes is crucial to avoid repeating them on the official exam.

5. **Study in Groups:**

   o Studying in a group can be very helpful, as it gives you the opportunity to discuss questions and answers with others. Often, explaining a concept to someone else can reinforce your understanding of that topic.

   o Sharing study materials and online resources with your study group can also offer new perspectives and enhance the learning process.

Stress Management

Taking the knowledge exam can be stressful, especially if it's your first time. However, with good stress management, you can maintain the calm and focus needed to successfully pass the exam.

Techniques for Staying Calm During the Exam

1. **Mental Preparation:**

   o Mental preparation is as important as academic preparation. Before the exam, visualize yourself successfully completing the test. This positive visualization technique can boost your confidence and reduce anxiety.

   o Remember that you have studied and are prepared. Focus on your knowledge and don't let doubts overwhelm you.

2. **Practice Deep Breathing:**

   o Deep breathing is a simple and effective technique for calming your nerves. Before and during the exam, take a few slow, deep breaths. Inhale deeply through your nose, hold your breath for a couple of seconds, then exhale slowly through your mouth. This helps relax your body and improve concentration.

3. **Manage Time During the Exam:**

   o During the exam, manage your time well. Don't spend too much time on a single question. If you're unsure of the answer, mark the question and move on; you can always come back to it later.

   o Read each question and all the answer options carefully before making your choice. Avoid rushing and take the time necessary to answer calmly.

4. **Avoid Excess Caffeine and Sugar:**

   o While it may seem like a good idea to have an energy drink before the exam, too much caffeine or sugar can increase anxiety. Instead, opt for a light, balanced meal before the exam that will provide energy without causing nervousness.

5. **Think Positively:**

- o Maintain a positive mindset. Remind yourself that you have the ability to pass the exam. Even if you encounter difficult questions, tackle them one at a time and stay confident in your abilities.

- o If you feel overwhelmed during the exam, take a moment to close your eyes, take a deep breath, and refocus your mind.

Passing the knowledge exam is an important step toward obtaining your driver's license. With good preparation and effective stress management, you will be able to approach the exam with confidence and success.

The Driving Test

Preparing for the Driving Test

The driving test is the final step toward obtaining a driver's license in Florida, and proper preparation is crucial to ensure you pass on your first attempt. This exam evaluates your practical driving skills and adherence to traffic laws, demonstrating that you are ready to drive safely and responsibly.

Tips on How to Prepare for the Practical Test

1. **Accumulate Sufficient Driving Experience:**

   o   Before taking the driving test, it's essential to accumulate a significant amount of practical driving experience. In Florida, learner's permit holders must complete at least 50 hours of supervised driving, with at least 10 hours of night driving.

   o   Try to drive in various conditions, including heavy traffic, nighttime driving, and adverse weather conditions such as rain or fog. This will help you feel comfortable in any situation you might encounter during the test.

2. **Familiarize Yourself with the Test Route:**

   o   Although test routes can vary, it's helpful to become familiar with the area around the DMV testing center where you will take the practical test. Know the main roads, intersections, and any residential areas that might be part of the route.

   o   If possible, practice driving in the area around the testing center. This will help you feel more confident and prepared on the day of the test.

3. **Practice Common Maneuvers:**

   o   During the driving test, you will be asked to perform a series of common maneuvers. These include parallel parking, reversing, making U-turns, changing lanes, and performing an emergency stop.

   o   Spend time practicing each of these maneuvers until you feel completely confident. Practice in an empty parking lot or a safe, quiet area where you can focus without distractions.

4. **Review the Rules of the Road:**

   o Although the driving test is primarily practical, the examiner will also assess your adherence to traffic laws. Be sure to review traffic laws, road signs, and specific Florida regulations, as discussed in previous chapters.

   o During the test, pay attention to all road signs and speed limits. Maintain a safe following distance from other vehicles and always use your turn signals when changing lanes or turning.

5. **Stay Calm and Focused:**

   o Mental preparation is as important as practical preparation. The driving test can be stressful, but try to stay calm and focused. Deep breathing and relaxation techniques can help you manage anxiety.

   o Remember that you have practiced all the maneuvers and are prepared for the test. Approach each stage with confidence and follow the examiner's instructions without rushing.

The Practical Test

The practical driving test is the moment when you will demonstrate your driving skills and knowledge of the road rules to the examiner. Understanding what to expect during the test can help you feel more prepared and reduce anxiety.

What to Expect During the Driving Test

1. **Before the Test Begins:**

   o When you arrive at the DMV testing center, the examiner will greet you and verify that all your documents are in order. This includes your learner's permit, vehicle registration, and insurance.

   o The examiner may ask you some preliminary questions to ensure you know the basic functions of the vehicle, such as turning on the lights, using the windshield wipers, and operating the horn. Make sure you know how to use all the vehicle controls.

2. **During the Test:**

   o The test usually begins with a series of basic maneuvers in a parking area or on a quiet street. These maneuvers may include parallel parking, reversing in a straight line, and controlled braking.

   o Next, the examiner will guide you on a route that may include residential streets, busy intersections, and stretches of road with higher speeds. Throughout the route, the examiner will assess your ability to follow traffic rules, manage traffic, and maintain control of the vehicle in various situations.

   o Pay attention to all of the examiner's instructions and respond promptly to their directions. Stay calm and drive as you have during your practice sessions.

3. **Common Maneuvers to Perform:**

   o **Parallel Parking:** You will be asked to perform a parallel parking maneuver between two vehicles or between cones. Be sure to signal before starting the maneuver and keep the vehicle well-aligned and at a proper distance from the curb.

   o **Reversing:** The examiner may ask you to reverse in a straight line over a short distance. Maintain control of the vehicle, constantly check behind you, and use your mirrors to ensure a safe maneuver.

   o **U-Turn:** This maneuver is required to assess your ability to make a complete turn without crossing into the opposite lane. Be sure to check for traffic and signal the turn before executing it.

   o **Emergency Stop:** You may be asked to perform a controlled stop to simulate an emergency situation. The examiner will evaluate your ability to brake safely and maintain control of the vehicle.

4. **Conclusion of the Test:**

   ○ At the end of the test, the examiner will ask you to return to the starting point. You will receive immediate feedback on your performance and be informed whether you passed or failed the test.

   ○ If you pass the test, the examiner will issue a temporary driver's license, valid until you receive the permanent license by mail. If you do not pass the test, the examiner will explain the errors you made, and you will be given the opportunity to retake the test in the future.

Passing the Driving Test

Passing the driving test requires not only technical skills but also the ability to stay calm and focused under pressure. By following some practical tips, you can significantly increase your chances of success.

Tips for Successfully Passing the Driving Test

1. **Stay Calm and Confident:**

   ○ It's normal to feel nervous during the driving test, but it's important to stay calm. Remember that the examiner is not there to make you fail but to ensure that you are ready to drive safely. Take deep breaths and focus on the road and your maneuvers.

   ○ Rely on your preparation. If you have accumulated driving experience and practiced the required maneuvers, you are well-equipped to pass the test.

2. **Follow the Examiner's Instructions:**

   ○ Listen carefully to the examiner's instructions and follow each direction precisely. If you don't understand an instruction, don't hesitate to ask for clarification. It's better to ask a question than to risk making a mistake.

   ○ Maintain an appropriate speed and always follow the rules of the road, even if the examiner doesn't explicitly ask. For example, make sure to come to a complete stop at a stop sign and check both ways before proceeding.

3. **Perform Maneuvers with Precision:**

   o During maneuvers, such as parallel parking or reversing, execute each movement calmly and precisely. Don't rush, and take the time you need to position the vehicle correctly.

   o Use your mirrors and constantly check your surroundings. Maintaining good situational awareness is crucial to avoiding mistakes during the test.

4. **Maintain a Safe Following Distance:**

   o One of the primary assessments during the test is your ability to maintain a safe following distance from other vehicles. Ensure that you keep a proper distance throughout the test, especially in heavy traffic areas or when following another vehicle.

   o Avoid driving too close to the vehicle in front of you and be ready to brake safely if necessary.

5. **Don't Let Minor Mistakes Distract You:**

   o If you make a small mistake during the test, don't let it discourage you. Continue driving calmly and with concentration. The examiner may overlook a minor error if you demonstrate the control and awareness necessary for safe driving.

   o Remember that the test evaluates your overall performance, not just a single moment. Even if you make a mistake, you can still pass the test if the rest of your driving is safe and compliant with the rules.

6. **Conclusion and Feedback:**

   o At the end of the test, listen carefully to the examiner's feedback. If you passed the test, congratulations! If you didn't pass, don't be discouraged. Use the feedback to improve your skills and retake the test with better preparation.

Traffic Rules

Traffic Laws in Florida

Florida's traffic laws are designed to ensure the safety of all road users, from drivers to pedestrians, and must be strictly followed to avoid accidents and penalties. These laws cover a wide range of situations and regulate everything from speed limits to proper intersection management and electronic device usage.

Overview of Major Traffic Laws in the State

1. **Speed Limits:**

   - In Florida, speed limits vary depending on the type of road and the area. In residential areas, the speed limit is usually 25-30 mph (about 40-48 km/h), while on interstate highways, the limit can reach up to 70 mph (about 112 km/h).

   - It is important to note that speed limits may be reduced near schools, in work zones, and in other areas where safety is a priority. These reduced limits are indicated by visible road signs and must be strictly observed.

2. **Right-of-Way Rules:**

   - Right-of-way rules in Florida determine who has the right to proceed in various traffic situations. For example, at intersections without traffic lights, the vehicle arriving from the right has the right of way. In roundabouts, vehicles already inside the roundabout have the right of way over those about to enter.

   - When making a left turn at an intersection, you must yield to oncoming vehicles going straight or turning right. Similarly, pedestrians always have the right of way at crosswalks.

3. **Seat Belt Usage:**

   - Seat belt use is mandatory in Florida for all vehicle occupants. The driver is responsible for ensuring that all passengers, both front and back, are properly buckled up. Seat belts are crucial in reducing the risk of serious injury in the event of an accident.

   - Children under the age of five must be secured in an appropriate child safety seat for their age and weight. Infants and young children must be placed in a rear-facing seat until they reach the weight or age recommended by the car seat manufacturer.

4. **Electronic Device Regulations:**

   - In Florida, texting while driving is prohibited. This is considered a primary offense, meaning police officers can stop you solely for this reason.

   - While using a cell phone for calls is not entirely prohibited, it is highly recommended to use a hands-free device to minimize distractions. The use of electronic devices is strictly forbidden in school zones and work zones.

5. **Pedestrian and Cyclist Regulations:**

   - Pedestrians must use sidewalks when available and cross streets only at crosswalks or regulated intersections. Drivers must yield to pedestrians at crosswalks, even if they are not marked by traffic signals.

   - Cyclists in Florida are required to follow the same traffic rules as motor vehicles and must travel in the same direction as traffic. Drivers must maintain a safe distance of at least three feet when passing a cyclist.

6. **Road Signs and Traffic Lights:**

   - Road signs regulate traffic flow and must be obeyed at all times. A stop sign requires a full stop, while a yield sign requires slowing down and giving way to approaching vehicles.

   - Traffic lights control intersections. A red light means you must come to a complete stop. In Florida, you may turn right on red after making a full stop and ensuring there are no oncoming vehicles or pedestrians.

Violations and Implications

Failing to comply with traffic laws in Florida can result in serious consequences, ranging from fines to license suspension, and even imprisonment in extreme cases. Understanding the various types of violations and their implications is essential for avoiding legal trouble and ensuring safe driving.

Types of Violations and Their Consequences

1. **Minor Violations:**

   o Minor violations include infractions such as slightly exceeding the speed limit, failing to use a seat belt, or not stopping fully at a stop sign. These infractions are generally punished with a fine and points deducted from your license.

   o For example, exceeding the speed limit by 10-14 mph typically results in a fine and the loss of 3 points on your license. Accumulating too many points in a short period can lead to a temporary suspension of your license.

2. **Serious Violations:**

   o Serious violations include behaviors such as driving under the influence of alcohol or drugs (DUI), driving without a license, or exceeding the speed limit by more than 30 mph. These infractions can result in hefty fines, license suspension or revocation, and in some cases, imprisonment.

   o DUI is one of the most severe violations. A first DUI offense can result in a fine of up to $1,000, imprisonment for up to six months, license suspension for at least 180 days, and mandatory installation of an Ignition Interlock Device.

3. **Criminal Offenses:**

   - Certain behaviors on the road can constitute criminal offenses, such as leaving the scene of an accident (hit and run), reckless driving causing serious injury or death, or participating in illegal street racing. These offenses are treated very seriously by the law and can result in significant prison sentences, permanent license revocation, and large fines.

   - For example, fleeing the scene of an accident that caused serious injury is a third-degree felony, punishable by up to 5 years in prison and a fine of up to $5,000.

4. **License Points Accumulation:**

   - In Florida, every traffic violation results in points being added to your driving record. Accumulating 12 points in 12 months can lead to a 30-day license suspension. Accumulating 18 points in 18 months can result in a 3-month suspension, and 24 points in 36 months can lead to a 1-year suspension.

   - It is important to monitor your point total and consider taking a safe driving course, which can help reduce accumulated points.

5. **Insurance Consequences:**

   - Traffic violations can significantly impact your insurance premiums. Insurance companies may increase premiums if a driver accumulates points on their license or is involved in accidents, especially if deemed at fault.

   - In some cases, a serious violation like a DUI can make it extremely difficult to obtain insurance at a reasonable cost and may require obtaining a high-risk policy.

Legal Updates

Traffic laws in Florida are periodically updated to reflect new safety needs, technological advancements, and trends in driver behavior. Keeping up to date with these changes is essential to ensure that you are always driving in compliance with the law.

Recent Changes to Traffic Regulations

1. **Restrictions on the Use of Electronic Devices:**

   o Recently, Florida has introduced stricter regulations on the use of electronic devices while driving. In addition to the ban on texting while driving, it is now illegal to hold a cell phone while driving in a school zone or work zone. Violations of these rules are considered primary offenses, allowing police officers to stop drivers solely for this reason.

   o These regulations have been implemented to reduce distractions while driving, which are a leading cause of road accidents.

2. **Updates to DUI Laws:**

   o DUI (Driving Under the Influence) laws have been strengthened with the introduction of harsher penalties for repeat offenders. For example, a second DUI offense within five years of the first can result in a license suspension for at least five years, imprisonment for up to nine months, and substantial fines.

   o Additionally, the use of Ignition Interlock Devices (IID) has been expanded, now requiring mandatory installation after a first DUI offense with a particularly high blood alcohol concentration (BAC).

3. **Cyclist Safety Laws:**

   o With the increasing number of cyclists on the roads, Florida has introduced new regulations to enhance the safety of these vulnerable road users. Drivers are now required to maintain a minimum distance of four feet when passing a cyclist and can be fined if they fail to observe this distance.

   o Urban areas with high cyclist density may also have reduced speed limits and specific signage to protect cyclists.

4. **School Zone Safety Initiatives:**

   o Regulations for school zone safety have been updated to include new protective measures. In addition to reduced speed limits, which must be strictly observed, new surveillance cameras have been installed to monitor vehicle speeds during school hours.

   o Drivers who violate speed limits in school zones now face much higher fines and the possibility of losing points on their license.

5. **Laws on Electric and Autonomous Vehicles:**

   o With the rise in the use of electric and autonomous vehicles, Florida has introduced new regulations to govern these types of vehicles. The new laws include specific requirements for registration, insurance, and the use of these vehicles on public roads.

   o For autonomous vehicles, the regulations require that the automated driving system meets the same safety standards as human drivers and that it can respond effectively to emergency situations.

QR Code Resources

We understand how important it is for you to have access to all the necessary information to best prepare for your driving license exam. To ensure that you can benefit from all the visual resources in color, we have decided to include a QR code in this book. Here's what you will find:

Access to Color Images

The images of road signs and other illustrations are crucial for your learning. Although this book is in black and white, we want to ensure that you can view these images in color. Scan the QR code provided to access the digital color version of the book.

How to Use the QR Code

Step 1: Open the camera app on your smartphone or use a QR code reader app.
Step 2: Point the camera at the QR code.
Step 3: Click on the link that appears to access the digital color version of the book.

Traffic Rules and Laws

Understanding and adhering to traffic rules and laws is essential for ensuring the safety of all road users. This chapter explores Florida traffic laws, parking regulations, DUI laws, and various violations and penalties.

Traffic Law Review

Florida's traffic laws are designed to maintain order and safety on the roads. Here are some of the most important laws:

Traffic Signs and Signals

- **Red Light:** Means STOP. You can turn right after stopping unless otherwise indicated. In Florida, a right turn on red is allowed after a complete stop unless a sign prohibits it.

- **Green Arrow:** Allows you to turn in the direction of the arrow, with a protected movement from other traffic.

- **Stop Signs:** Stop completely before entering an intersection or stop line. Ensure the intersection is clear before proceeding.

Right-of-Way Rules

- **Pedestrians:** Pedestrians always have the right of way at crosswalks. Florida law requires drivers to yield to pedestrians in marked crosswalks and intersections without traffic signals.

- **Uncontrolled Intersections:** The vehicle that arrives first has the right of way. If two vehicles arrive simultaneously, the vehicle on the right has the right of way.

Speed Limits

- **Speed Limits:** Speed limits are set for safety. In residential areas and near schools, the typical limit is 25-30 mph unless otherwise posted. On highways, speed limits can range from 55 to 70 mph depending on the area.

- **Speeding:** Exceeding the speed limit can result in fines and points on your license. Florida uses a point system where accumulating too many points can lead to license suspension.

Lane Usage

- **Passing Lane:** The leftmost lane is typically used for passing other vehicles. However, Florida law also prohibits prolonged travel in the left lane if it impedes the flow of traffic.

- **Reserved Lanes (HOV):** Reserved for vehicles with multiple passengers, buses, and motorcycles during specific hours.

Emergency Vehicles

- **Yielding:** It is mandatory to yield to emergency vehicles with lights and sirens on, pulling over to the right and stopping if necessary. Failure to do so can result in significant penalties.

Parking Laws

Parking is regulated by specific laws that vary depending on the location and type of area. Here are some of the main parking laws in Florida:

Parking Zones

- **Red Zone:** Typically indicates no parking allowed, similar to many states.

- **Yellow Zone:** Loading and unloading permitted only for a short period.

- **White Zone:** Stopping allowed for picking up or dropping off passengers.

Disabled Parking

- Only vehicles with a disabled permit or license plate can park in spaces reserved for the disabled. Violations result in fines of $250 or more.

Parking Prohibitions

- It is illegal to park near intersections, crosswalks, bus stops, and fire hydrants.

- Parking on sidewalks or in a way that blocks traffic is prohibited.

Signage and Signals

- Always comply with vertical and horizontal signage regulating parking. Fines for parking violations can range from $35 to $100, depending on the severity of the violation.

Driving Under the Influence (DUI): Laws and Penalties

Driving under the influence of alcohol or drugs is severely punished in Florida. DUI laws and penalties are designed to deter drivers from operating a vehicle while impaired and to protect public safety.

Blood Alcohol Content (BAC) Limits

- For drivers aged 21 and older, the legal BAC limit is 0.08%.

- For drivers under 21, the limit is 0.02%, significantly lower due to zero-tolerance policies.

Number of Drinks		Body Weight in Pounds								Driving Condition
		100	120	140	160	180	200	220	240	
0	M	.00	.00	.00	.00	.00	.00	.00	.00	Only Safe Driving Limit
	F	.00	.00	.00	.00	.00	.00	.00	.00	
1	M	.06	.05	.04	.04	.03	.03	.03	.02	Driving Skills Impaired
	F	.07	.06	.05	.04	.04	.03	.03	.03	
2	M	.12	.10	.09	.07	.07	.06	.05	.05	
	F	.13	.11	.09	.08	.07	.07	.06	.06	
3	M	.18	.15	.13	.11	.10	.09	.08	.07	Legally Intoxicated
	F	.20	.17	.14	.12	.11	.10	.09	.08	
4	M	.24	.20	.17	.15	.13	.12	.11	.10	
	F	.26	.22	.19	.17	.15	.13	.12	.11	
5	M	.30	.25	.21	.19	.17	.15	.14	.12	
	F	.33	.28	.24	.21	.18	.17	.15	.14	

BLOOD ALCOHOL CONTENT (BAC)
Table for Male (M) / Female (F)

Subtract .01% for each 40 minutes that lapse between drinks.
1 drink = 1.5 oz. 80 proof liquor, 12 oz. 5% beer, or 5 oz. 12% wine.
Fewer than 5 persons out of 100 will exceed these values.

DUI Penalties

- **First Offense:** Fines up to $1,000, license suspension for 180 days, and possible incarceration for up to six months.

- **Second Offense:** Fines up to $2,000, license suspension for one year, and incarceration from 10 days to nine months.

- **Multiple Offenses:** Fines up to $5,000, license suspension for up to 10 years, and incarceration for up to five years.

Implied Consent Law

- Driving in Florida implies consent to submit to alcohol or drug tests if requested by a police officer. Refusal results in an automatic license suspension for one year and a fine.

Violations and Penalties: From Minor Infractions to Major Offenses

Traffic law violations can range from minor infractions to major offenses, each with specific penalties.

Minor Infractions

- **Fine:** Minor violations, such as slightly exceeding the speed limit or failing to stop at a stop sign, result in fines ranging from $35 to $250 and points on the driver's license.

- **Points on License:** Each infraction adds points to the driver's record. Accumulating too many points can lead to license suspension.

Misdemeanor Offenses

- **Reckless Driving:** Behaviors such as reckless driving can result in fines up to $1,000 and imprisonment for up to six months.

- **DUI:** As discussed, DUI is considered a misdemeanor but carries heavy penalties.

Felony Offenses

- **DUI with Injuries:** Causing an accident with injuries while under the influence can result in fines up to $5,000, imprisonment from one to five years, and license revocation.

- **Evading Police:** Attempting to evade a police officer in a vehicle is a felony with penalties of six months to one year in prison and fines up to $10,000.

Points on License and Suspensions

- Accumulating 12 points in 12 months, 18 points in 18 months, or 24 points in 36 months can lead to license suspension. Participation in a hearing may be required to contest the suspension.

Implied Consent Law

Driving in California implies consent to submit to alcohol or drug tests if requested by a police officer. Refusal results in an automatic license suspension for one year and a $125 fine.

Violations and Penalties: From Minor Infractions to Major Offenses

Traffic law violations can range from minor infractions to major offenses, each with specific penalties.

Minor Infractions

- **Fine**: Minor violations, such as slightly exceeding the speed limit or failing to stop at a stop sign, result in fines ranging from $35 to $250 and points on the driver's license.

- **Points on License**: Each infraction adds points to the driver's record. Accumulating too many points can lead to license suspension.

Misdemeanor Offenses

- **Reckless Driving**: Behaviors such as reckless driving can result in fines up to $1,000 and imprisonment for up to six months.

- **DUI**: As discussed, DUI is considered a misdemeanor but carries heavy penalties.

Felony Offenses

- **DUI with Injuries**: Causing an accident with injuries while under the influence can result in fines up to $5,000, imprisonment from one to 16 months, and license revocation.

- **Evading Police**: Attempting to evade a police officer in a vehicle is a felony with penalties of six months to one year in prison and fines up to $10,000.

Points on License and Suspensions

- Accumulating 4 points in 12 months, 6 points in 24 months, or 8 points in 36 months can lead to license suspension. Participation in a hearing may be required to contest the suspension.

Road signs

Traffic signage is a crucial component of road safety. Traffic signs convey vital information that helps drivers navigate safely and efficiently. This chapter will provide a comprehensive overview of the different types of traffic signs, explain the colors and shapes used, and discuss the importance and function of these signs.

Types of traffic signs

Traffic signs in California can be divided into three main categories: regulatory signs, warning signs, and guide signs.

Regulatory Signs

Stop
Instructs drivers to come to a complete stop at the limit line, crosswalk, or before entering the intersection. Essential for road safety and right-of-way compliance.

Yield
Instructs drivers to slow down and, if necessary, stop to give the right of way to other vehicles or pedestrians. Ensures safe and orderly traffic flow at intersections.

Do Not Enter
Instructs drivers not to enter a road or area, typically because it is a one-way street in the opposite direction. Helps prevent accidents and ensure proper traffic flow.

No U-Turn Sign
Informs drivers that U-turns are prohibited. Placed in areas where making a U-turn could be dangerous or disrupt the flow of traff

Regulatory Signs (Black and White)

Speed Limit Sign
Tells you the maximum speed allowed by law on thehighways or roadway that you are driving on

Keep Right Signs
Indicate that the vehicles must keep to right side to avoid a divideror an obstacle.

Keep Left Signs
Indicate that the vehicles must keep to left side to avoid a divideror an obstacle.

One-Way Signs
Marks a one-way street; arrowpoints in the direction that the traffic flows.

Traffic Warning Signs

Warning signs inform drivers of unforeseen or dangerous conditions requiring reduced speed or other safety actions. These signs, often yellow or orange with black symbols or letters, are typically diamond-shaped or rectangular. Yellow pennant-shaped signs indicate where passing is unsafe, while round yellow signs alert drivers to an upcoming railroad crossing.

Turn With Advisory Speed Limit

Indicates a left turn with a recommended maximum speed for safe navigation. Displays a left-curving arrow and a number representing the advisory speed.

Chevron Left Sign

Indicates a sharp or hazardous left turn. Features arrows angled left on a yellow or orange background, helping drivers to slow down and take the turn cautiously.

Speed Reduction Ahead Sign

Indicates an upcoming speed reduction. Warns drivers to slow down before a change in the speed limit.

Slow Warning

Warns drivers to slow down. Used in areas where caution is needed due to road conditions or upcoming hazards.

Hill with grade Sign
Indicates a steep hill with a specific grade percentage. Warns drivers to prepare for challenging driving conditions and adjust their speed accordingly.

Slippery When Wet
Warns drivers that the road becomes slippery when wet. Indicates to reduce speed and drive carefully in rainy or humid conditions.

No Passing Zone
Indicates an area where passing is prohibited. Typically placed on roads with curves, hills, or other conditions that make passing dangerous.

Workers Symbol Sign
Indicates an upcoming speed reduction. Warns drivers to slow down before a change in the speed limit.

Street Closed
Warns drivers to slow down. Used in areas where caution is needed due to road conditions or upcoming hazards.

Parking Signs

Parking signs are essential for guiding drivers on where and when they can park, as well as indicating areas where parking is prohibited. These signs provide crucial information to avoid fines, ensure safety, and maintain order in urban and rural areas. Parking signs clearly indicate:

Where You Can Park:

They specify designated parking areas, such as public parking lots, paid parking areas, and roadside parking spots. These signs help drivers find safe and authorized parking spaces, thus avoiding reserved or hazardous areas.

When You Can Park:

They provide information on the permitted parking times. For instance, some signs allow parking only during certain hours of the day or night, or prohibit parking during street cleaning days or special events.

Where You Cannot Park:

They indicate areas where parking is prohibited for safety, accessibility, or local regulation reasons. This includes loading/unloading zones, resident-only areas, bus stops, driveways, and points near intersections that must remain clear to ensure visibility and road safety.

Railroad Crossing Signs

Railroad crossing signs are designed to inform drivers that they are approaching a railroad crossing.

These signs are crucial for ensuring road safety by alerting motorists to the presence of railway tracks and the potential for trains to cross the road.

Their presence signals drivers to slow down, pay extra attention, and be prepared to stop if necessary. Railroad crossing signs may include flashing lights, warning sounds, and barriers that lower when a train is approaching, providing a clear and timely warning to prevent accidents

Road_Colors

 **Red**
The color red on traffic signs indicates a prohibition or a requirement. It is used to signal actions that drivers must stop or avoid, such as coming to a complete stop or not entering.

 Yellow
The color yellow on traffic signs warns drivers of potentially hazardous or unexpected conditions that require attention. It is used to signal curves, intersections, lane changes, and other upcoming dangers.

 Green
The color green on traffic signs provides guidance and direction information. It is used to indicate destinations, distances, highway exits, and other useful navigation information.

 **Blue**
The color blue on traffic signs provides information about road services, tourist facilities, and recreational areas. It is used to indicate hospitals, rest areas, gas stations, restaurants, and other traveler support facilities.

 **Black and White**
The colors white and black on traffic signs are used to indicate regulations and traffic laws. These signs provide information on speed limits, driving directions, parking regulations, and other rules that drivers must follow.

Shapes Of Road Signs

Octagonal Sign

The octagonal shape is used exclusively for the "Stop" sign. It requires drivers to come to a complete stop and ensures maximum visibility and recognizability.

Triangular Sign

The triangular shape, with the point facing downward, is used for the "Yield" sign. It instructs drivers to slow down and, if necessary, stop to give the right of way to other vehicles.

Rectangular Sign

The rectangular shape is primarily used for informational, regulatory, and guide signs. It provides information on speed limits, parking regulations, directions, and road services.

Diamond Shape Sign

The diamond shape is used for warning signs. It indicates potentially hazardous or unexpected road conditions that require drivers' attention, such as curves, intersections, road work, and lane changes.

Circular Sign

The circular shape is primarily used for railroad crossing signs. It informs drivers that they should prepare to stop and yield to any approaching trains

No Turn Signs

No turn signs are essential traffic signage designed to prevent drivers from making illegal maneuvers.

These signs specifically prohibit left turns, right turns, or U-turns, which could jeopardize road safety.

They are commonly placed at intersections to clearly indicate that such maneuvers are not allowed. Additionally, no turn signs are often used at one-way street intersections to reinforce the prohibition of turns in the opposite direction. These signs are typically white and black, featuring a diagonal red slash across the symbol of the prohibited turn, making them easily recognizable and understandable for all road users.

No Left Turn

No Right Turn

No U Turn

Importance and Function of Traffic Signs

Traffic signs play crucial roles in ensuring road safety and efficiency.

Clear Communication

- Traffic signs provide essential information clearly and concisely, reducing the possibility of misunderstandings and increasing safety.

Traffic Regulation

- They help regulate traffic flow, preventing accidents and ensuring that drivers comply with traffic laws.

Navigation

- Guide signs assist drivers in navigation, indicating directions, highway exits, and points of interest.

Accident Prevention

- Warning signs alert drivers to potential hazards, allowing them to adjust their driving and prevent accidents.

Driver Education

- Traffic signs educate new drivers on the rules of the road and reinforce the knowledge of experienced drivers

Pavement Markings Explained

Pavement markings provide guidance to drivers about road usage, upcoming conditions, and where passing is permitted. Symbols indicate allowed lane usage, such as diamonds for high-occupancy vehicles and bicycles for bike lanes. Markings also warn drivers about hazardous conditions, such as railroad crossings and speed bumps. Drivers should stay within lane markings unless they are turning, exiting a highway, or changing lanes.

Edge lines are solid lines drawn along the sides of the road that define the right or left boundary of the roadway.

Single Solid White EdgeLine
Marks the right edge of the roadway.

Single Solid Yellow EdgeLine
Marks the left edge of the roadway on dividedhighways and one-way streets.

White Lane Lines separate traffic moving in the *same direction.*

Single Broken White Line
A single broken white line separates lanes of traffic moving in the same direction. It indicates that lane changes are allowed, but drivers should do so with caution and ensure it is safe before making the move.

Single Solid White Line
A single solid white line separates lanes of traffic moving in the same direction. It indicates that drivers should avoid changing lanes unless necessary due to emergencies. It is used to discourage lane changes at hazardous locations, such as near intersections.

Double Solid White Lines

Double solid white lines separate lanes of traffic moving in the *same direction*. They indicate that lane changes are prohibited. Drivers must stay in their lane and not cross the lines.

Yellow Lane Lines separate traffic moving in *opposite directions*.

Double Solid Yellow Lines

Double solid yellow lines separate traffic moving in *opposite directions*. They indicate that passing is prohibited in both directions. Drivers must stay in their lane and not cross the lines.

Broken Yellow Line

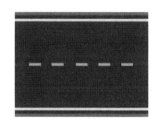

The broken yellow line separates traffic moving in *opposite directions*. It indicates that passing is allowed if it is safe to do so. Drivers must ensure that the road is clear of oncoming traffic before making a pass.

Types of Traffic Lights

Traffic lights manage the flow of traffic at intersections and in other situations. These devices are essential for preventing accidents and maintaining order.

.

<u>Red Traffic Light</u>

.

A red traffic light signals drivers to come to a complete stop at the stop line or corner of the intersection. It is a mandatory stop signal designed to ensure safety and orderly traffic flow. Drivers must wait until the light turns green and the intersection is clear and safe before proceeding.

Yellow Traffic Light

A yellow traffic light warns drivers that the light is about to turn red. It signals to slow down and prepare to stop if it is safe to do so. If stopping safely is not possible, drivers should proceed through the intersection with caution.

Green Traffic Light

A green traffic light signals drivers that they may proceed through the intersection. However, they must always yield to pedestrians and vehicles still in the intersection. When turning left, drivers must yield to oncoming traffic and pedestrians.

Pedestrian Signals

Pedestrian signals indicate when it is safe for pedestrians to cross the street. They usually display a walking person (WALK) to indicate it is safe to cross and an upraised hand (DON'T WALK) to indicate it is not safe to cross. Some signals include a countdown timer showing how much time is left to cross safely.

WALK

The WALK signal, shown by a walking person, tells pedestrians it is safe to cross the street. Pedestrians can start crossing but should watch for turning vehicles.

DON'T WALK

The DON'T WALK signal, shown by an upraised hand, indicates to pedestrians that it is not safe to cross the street. Pedestrians should wait for the WALK signal before starting to cross.

Countdown Signal.
The countdown signal displays a timer that indicates to pedestrians how much time is left to safely cross the street. When the countdown is active, pedestrians should complete crossing before the time runs out.

Pedestrian Crossing.

The pedestrian crossing sign marks a specific area where pedestrians can safely cross the street. Typically accompanied by road markings and sometimes flashing lights, it alerts drivers to slow down and stop to allow pedestrians to cross.

School Zone

Slow down to 20 mph or slower, watch for children crossing the street, and be prepared to stop. Look for school safety patrols or crossing guards and obey their directions at all times. In Florida, the speed limit is 20 mph within 500 to 1,000 feet of a school when children are present, whether they are outside, crossing the street, or waiting at a school bus stop. Some school zones may have speed limits as low as 15 mph, and these limits are strictly enforced during posted hours.

Safe Driving Techniques

Good Driving Habits

Good driving habits are crucial for ensuring your safety and that of other road users. Adopting safe and responsible behaviors significantly reduces the risk of accidents and helps create a safer driving environment for everyone.

Behaviors That Promote Road Safety

1. **Stay Focused on the Road:**

   o One of the leading causes of road accidents is distraction. Avoid using your cell phone, adjusting the radio, or engaging in any activities that could divert your attention from driving. Focus on the road and be aware of other vehicles, pedestrians, and cyclists around you.

   o Keep both hands on the wheel and your eyes on the road. If you need to use an electronic device, pull over to a safe location before doing so.

2. **Observe Speed Limits:**

   o Speed limits are set to ensure safety under various road and environmental conditions. Adhering to these limits reduces the risk of accidents and gives you more time to react to unexpected situations.

   o Remember that speed limits are not just maximums; in some situations, such as during adverse weather conditions, it may be safer to drive at a lower speed than the posted limit.

3. **Maintain a Safe Following Distance:**

   o Keeping a safe distance from the vehicle in front of you is essential to avoid rear-end collisions. A general rule is the "three-second rule": choose a fixed point on the road and ensure at least three seconds pass between when the vehicle ahead passes that point and when you do.

   o In low visibility conditions or on slippery roads, increase this distance to allow more reaction time.

4. **Use Turn Signals:**

   o Signaling your intentions to other drivers is crucial for preventing accidents. Always use your turn signals when changing lanes, turning at intersections, or entering a roundabout.

   o Activate the signal well in advance to give other drivers time to react. Remember to turn off the signal after completing your maneuver.

5. **Avoid Aggressive Driving:**

   o Aggressive driving behaviors, such as cutting off other drivers, sudden acceleration, or tailgating, greatly increase the risk of accidents. Maintaining calm and patience is essential, especially in heavy traffic.

   o If you encounter an aggressive driver, avoid responding in kind. Keep a safe distance and, if necessary, allow them to pass.

6. **Don't Drive Under the Influence:**

   o Driving under the influence of alcohol or drugs is extremely dangerous and illegal. Even small amounts of alcohol can impair your reflexes and judgment.

   o If you've been drinking or taking medications that could affect your driving, arrange for a sober friend to drive, use public transportation, or take a ride-sharing service.

7. **Ensure You're Well-Rested:**

   o Fatigue can be just as dangerous as intoxication. If you feel tired, stop in a safe area to take a break or have some coffee. Avoid driving long distances without rest.

   o If possible, share the driving with a passenger so you can alternate and rest.

Adapting to Road Conditions

The ability to adapt your driving to road conditions is crucial for maintaining safety. Road conditions can vary significantly depending on weather, environment, and traffic, and knowing how to respond to these changes can prevent accidents.

How to Adapt Driving Based on Road Conditions

1. **Driving on Wet or Slippery Roads:**

   o Wet roads, especially after a light rain, can become very slippery due to the buildup of oil and dirt on the road surface. Reduce your speed and increase the following distance from the vehicle in front of you.

   o Avoid sudden braking or sharp maneuvers. Use gentle and gradual steering inputs to maintain control of the vehicle.

2. **Night Driving:**

   o Night driving presents unique challenges, such as reduced visibility and glare from other vehicles' headlights. Keep your headlights clean and ensure they are properly aligned to maximize visibility without blinding other drivers.

   o Reduce speed and use high beams only when there are no oncoming vehicles. If you are blinded by the headlights of an oncoming vehicle, glance slightly to the right to avoid being dazzled.

3. **Driving in Urban Areas:**

   o Urban areas are often characterized by heavy traffic, pedestrians, cyclists, and multiple traffic signals. Drive cautiously, reduce speed, and pay close attention to traffic signs and signals.

   o Be particularly mindful of pedestrians, especially near schools and parks. Remember that pedestrians always have the right of way at crosswalks.

4. **Driving in Rural Areas:**

   o   In rural areas, you may encounter narrow roads, blind curves, and wildlife crossing the road. Reduce speed and be prepared to stop at any time.

   o   Use high beams at night to improve visibility, but dim them when approaching another vehicle. Be alert for signs indicating the presence of wildlife and slow down in these areas.

5. **Driving in Heavy Traffic:**

   o   In heavy traffic, it is essential to stay calm and drive cautiously. Avoid frequent lane changes and maintain a safe following distance.

   o   Anticipate the movements of other drivers and be prepared to stop safely if traffic suddenly slows down. Use your mirrors frequently to stay aware of what is happening around you.

6. **Driving on Mountain Roads:**

   o   Mountain roads can be particularly challenging due to tight curves, steep grades, and changing weather conditions. Use a lower gear to control your speed on downhill stretches and reduce speed before entering curves.

   o   Be aware of the risk of falling rocks and wildlife crossing the road. Avoid prolonged brake use to prevent overheating.

Driving in Adverse Conditions

Driving in challenging weather conditions requires increased attention and preparation. Whether it's rain, fog, snow, or strong winds, adjusting your driving style to these conditions can make the difference between a safe journey and an accident.

Tips for Safe Driving in Difficult Weather Conditions

1. **Driving in Rain:**

   o Rain is one of the most common and hazardous weather conditions for driving. When it starts to rain, roads become slippery due to the accumulation of oil and dirt. Reduce your speed and turn on your headlights to improve visibility.

   o Avoid puddles, which can cause hydroplaning, a situation where your tires lose contact with the road. If this happens, stay calm, reduce speed, and avoid sudden steering movements.

2. **Driving in Fog:**

   o Fog can drastically reduce visibility and make it difficult to judge distances between vehicles. Turn on your fog lights if your vehicle is equipped with them, and drive at a reduced speed.

   o Use the road's edge markings as a guide and increase your following distance from the vehicle in front. Avoid using high beams, as the light reflected in the fog can further reduce visibility.

3. **Driving in Snow or Ice:**

   o While snow and ice are less common in Florida, they can still occur in some areas during winter. If you find yourself driving in these conditions, drastically reduce your speed and use lower gears to maintain control of your vehicle.

   o Avoid sudden maneuvers and maintain a much greater following distance than usual. Remember that stopping distances on snow or ice are significantly longer.

4. **Driving in Strong Winds:**

   o   Strong winds can affect vehicle control, especially on bridges or in open areas. Keep both hands firmly on the steering wheel and reduce your speed to maintain control.

   o   Be particularly cautious when passing large vehicles like trucks or buses, as they are more susceptible to wind effects.

5. **Prepare for Emergencies:**

   o   Before setting out in adverse conditions, ensure that your vehicle is in good condition, with appropriate tires and functioning brakes. Always keep an emergency kit in your vehicle, including items like a flashlight, blankets, water, and jumper cables.

   o   In case of an emergency, remain calm and try to move your vehicle to a safe spot off the road. If you need to stop, turn on your hazard lights to alert other drivers to your presence.

Driver Responsibility

Legal and Moral Responsibilities

Being a driver comes with a series of legal and moral responsibilities. These obligations are essential to ensure the safety of oneself and others on the road. Every driver must be aware of their actions and the potential consequences they may have.

Obligations of the Driver Toward Themselves and Others

1. **Compliance with Traffic Laws:**

   - Every driver is legally obligated to follow traffic laws. This includes adhering to speed limits, obeying traffic signals and signs, and following rules regarding overtaking and right-of-way.

   - Failure to comply with these laws not only exposes the driver to legal penalties but also puts the lives and safety of all road users at risk.

2. **Defensive Driving:**

   - Defensive driving involves anticipating potential hazards and being prepared to respond safely. This approach reduces the risk of accidents caused by one's own or others' mistakes.

   - A defensive driver is always aware of road conditions, the behavior of other drivers, and any obstacles or hazards along the route.

3. **Moral Responsibility:**

   - Beyond legal responsibilities, drivers have a moral obligation to drive safely and respectfully. This includes respecting the lives and safety of others on the road, whether they are other drivers, pedestrians, or cyclists.

   - Moral responsibility also extends to avoiding behaviors that could endanger others, such as distracted driving, driving under the influence, or failing to maintain a safe following distance.

4. **Maintaining Your Vehicle:**

   - A well-maintained vehicle is crucial for road safety. It is the driver's responsibility to ensure that the vehicle is in good working condition, with properly functioning brakes, lights, tires, and other critical components.

   - Regular maintenance and inspections reduce the risk of mechanical failures that could lead to accidents.

5. **Ethical Conduct in Case of an Accident:**

   - In the event of an accident, drivers have a legal and moral obligation to stop immediately, provide assistance if possible, and exchange information with other parties involved. Fleeing the scene of an accident is a serious crime with severe legal consequences.

   - Even if there are no injuries, it is important to exchange information with other drivers and, if necessary, contact authorities for an official report.

Auto Insurance

Auto insurance is a legal requirement for all drivers in Florida and is a crucial element of driver responsibility. Insurance not only protects the driver from the financial consequences of accidents but also ensures that accident victims receive adequate compensation.

Types of Insurance Coverage and Requirements in Florida

1. **Liability Insurance:**

   - Liability insurance is the basic type of coverage required by law in Florida. This coverage protects the driver from claims for bodily injury or property damage caused to others in an accident where they are found to be at fault.

   - Florida law requires a minimum coverage of $10,000 for bodily injury liability and $10,000 for property damage liability. However, it is advisable to carry higher coverage amounts for greater financial protection.

2. **Personal Injury Protection (PIP):**

   o In Florida, PIP is mandatory and covers medical expenses for the driver and passengers, regardless of who is at fault in the accident. This coverage also includes lost wages and other costs associated with injuries.

   o PIP provides a minimum coverage of $10,000, but higher coverage can be purchased for added financial security in case of serious accidents.

3. **Uninsured/Underinsured Motorist Coverage:**

   o This coverage protects the driver in the event of an accident with another driver who does not have insurance or has insufficient coverage to pay for damages.

   o Although this insurance is not mandatory in Florida, it is strongly recommended to ensure that you are protected even in situations where the other driver cannot cover the costs.

4. **Comprehensive and Collision Insurance:**

   o Collision insurance covers damage to your vehicle in the event of an accident, regardless of who is at fault. Comprehensive insurance covers damages caused by non-collision events, such as theft, vandalism, or natural disasters.

   o While not mandatory, this coverage is often required by lenders if the vehicle is financed or leased.

5. **Commercial Auto Insurance:**

   o Vehicles used for commercial purposes, such as freight transportation or ride-sharing services, require specific insurance coverage. This coverage is more comprehensive and takes into account the more intensive use of the vehicle.

   o Businesses and independent drivers using their vehicles for commercial purposes must ensure they have adequate coverage to protect themselves from potential high liabilities.

Consequences of Irresponsibility

Failing to uphold legal and moral responsibilities as a driver can lead to severe consequences, both legally and financially. It is crucial to understand the implications of irresponsible behavior on the road and how it can affect your life and the lives of others.

Implications of Irresponsible Behavior on the Road

1. **Legal Penalties:**

   o   Traffic violations can result in fines, loss of points on your license, and even the suspension or revocation of your driver's license. Serious offenses, such as driving under the influence (DUI) of alcohol or drugs, can lead to imprisonment.

   o   Accumulating points on your license can lead to automatic suspension. In Florida, accumulating 12 points within 12 months can result in a 30-day suspension, while 18 points within 18 months can lead to a three-month suspension.

2. **Financial Consequences:**

   o   In addition to legal penalties, traffic violations can have significant financial consequences. Fines can be very steep, especially for serious offenses like DUI.

   o   Additionally, insurance premiums can rise sharply following accidents or traffic violations. Insurance companies consider drivers with poor driving records as high-risk, which is reflected in higher premiums.

3. **Civil Liability:**

   o   In the event of an accident caused by irresponsible behavior, the driver may be civilly liable for the damages caused. This can include compensation for property damage, medical expenses, loss of income, and even emotional distress.

   o   In severe cases, claims for compensation can exceed insurance coverage, leaving the driver personally responsible for paying the remainder with their personal assets.

4. **Impact on Reputation and Career:**

   o A poor driving record can negatively impact your reputation and career, especially if your job requires the use of a vehicle. Some employers may refuse to hire or retain an employee with a problematic driving record.

   o Additionally, a suspended or revoked license can limit your job opportunities, particularly in fields that require a valid license.

5. **Risks to Life and Safety:**

   o The most severe consequence of irresponsible driving is the risk to life and safety. Behaviors such as distracted driving, speeding, or driving under the influence can lead to fatal accidents.

   o Protecting your life and the lives of others should always be the top priority. Every time you get behind the wheel, remember the importance of driving responsibly and with respect for others.

Final Preparation for the Exam

Tips and Techniques for the Exam

Facing the final exam to obtain your driver's license can be stressful, but proper preparation and effective techniques can make the difference between success and failure. This section provides practical advice on how to approach the exam with confidence and competence.

Tips on How to Approach the Final Exam

1. **Familiarize Yourself with the Exam Route:**

   o   If possible, find out about the test route you might encounter. Some DMV offices use predetermined routes for the driving exam. Practicing on these routes, if known, can help you become familiar with critical areas and required maneuvers.

   o   Even if the route is not known, practice driving in the vicinity of the DMV to get used to local traffic, road signs, and road conditions.

2. **Review Traffic Rules:**

   o   Before the exam, review the key traffic rules, road signs, and specific Florida laws. This will help you quickly and correctly respond to any theoretical questions that might be asked during the practical exam.

   o   Focus on less common or complex rules, such as roundabout management, right-of-way rules, and school zone laws.

3. **Practice Basic Maneuvers:**

   o   Make sure you are completely comfortable with the basic maneuvers required during the exam, such as parallel parking, backing up, lane changes, and U-turns. Practicing these maneuvers repeatedly will help you execute them confidently during the exam.

   o   Don't neglect less common maneuvers, such as emergency stops or straight-line reversing. These might be evaluated during the exam and require precision.

4. **Maintain Smooth and Safe Driving:**

   o During the exam, avoid abrupt or sudden maneuvers. Drive smoothly and safely, maintaining a consistent speed and always obeying speed limits. Use turn signals well in advance and always check your mirrors before changing lanes or turning.

   o The smoothness of your driving demonstrates to the examiner that you are a safe and competent driver.

5. **Prepare All Necessary Documents:**

   o Before heading to the exam, ensure you have all required documents, such as your learner's permit, vehicle insurance, and appointment confirmation. The absence of documents could prevent you from taking the exam.

   o Organize your documents neatly and present them promptly when requested by the examiner.

6. **Arrive Early and Well-Rested:**

   o Make sure to arrive at the DMV well before your appointment time. This will give you time to relax and mentally prepare for the exam.

   o The night before the exam, try to get a good night's sleep to be rested and focused. Fatigue can negatively impact your performance during the exam.

Practice Tests

Practice is one of the best ways to prepare for the final exam. Practice tests can help you identify any areas where you need improvement and give you a clear idea of what to expect during the actual exam.

Exercises to Simulate the Official Exam

1. **Practical Driving Exercises:**

   o Conduct practical driving exercises on routes that closely mimic the test route. Ask a friend or family member to act as an "examiner" and evaluate your driving according to the criteria that will be used during the official exam.

   o Focus on key maneuvers required during the exam, such as parallel parking, reversing, and handling complex intersections. Be mindful of obeying all traffic rules during these exercises.

2. **Evaluate Your Performance:**

   o After each practice session, take the time to assess your performance. Identify areas where you made mistakes or feel less confident and repeat those maneuvers until you can perform them effortlessly.

   o Seek honest feedback from the person who observed you during practice. An external perspective can help you see aspects of your driving that you might have overlooked.

Managing Stress

Stress can negatively affect your performance during the exam, so it's important to adopt strategies to stay calm and focused. This section offers techniques for managing stress before and during the exam.

Strategies for Staying Calm During the Exam

1. **Mental Preparation:**

   o   Mentally preparing for the exam is crucial. Visualize yourself successfully and calmly completing the exam. This visualization technique can help build your confidence and reduce anxiety.

   o   Remember that the exam is an opportunity to demonstrate your skills, not something to be feared. Focus on your abilities and your preparation.

2. **Breathing Techniques:**

   o   Deep breathing is an effective method for calming nerves. If you feel stressed before or during the exam, take a few deep, slow breaths. Inhale deeply through your nose, hold your breath for a moment, and then exhale slowly through your mouth.

   o   This technique helps to lower your heart rate and calm your mind, allowing you to approach the exam with greater clarity.

3. **Time Management:**

   o   During the exam, manage your time well. Don't rush, and take the necessary time to execute each maneuver carefully and precisely. If you find yourself in a difficult situation, pause for a moment to think before acting.

   o   If the exam includes a theoretical portion, read each question and all the answer options carefully before making your choice. Avoid answering impulsively and take the time to reflect.

4. **Maintain a Positive Mindset:**

   o A positive mindset can make a big difference. Remind yourself that you've prepared and are capable of passing the exam. Even if you encounter a difficult question or a tricky maneuver, maintain confidence in your abilities.

   o If you make a mistake during the exam, don't let it discourage you. Continue to focus on the rest of the exam and do your best to correct any errors.

5. **Acknowledge and Accept Anxiety:**

   o It's normal to feel anxious before an important exam. Acknowledge this anxiety as a normal part of the process and don't let it overwhelm you. Accepting anxiety can reduce its impact, allowing you to focus better.

   o Talk to friends or family members who have already passed the driving exam for support and advice. Knowing that others have successfully gone through the same experience can help you feel less alone and more prepared.

Traffic Rules Quiz

1. What is the speed limit in a residential area in Florida?
A) 20 mph
B) 25 mph
C) 30 mph
D) 35 mph

2. When is it allowed to turn right at a red traffic light?
A) Never
B) After making a complete stop and if there are no signs prohibiting it
C) Only if the light is flashing
D) Always

3. What is the minimum following distance you should maintain from the vehicle in front of you?
A) Two seconds
B) Three seconds
C) Four seconds
D) Five seconds

4. Which sign indicates that you must come to a complete stop?
A) Yield sign
B) Stop sign
C) Green traffic light
D) Parking sign

5. What does a traffic signal with a green arrow mean?
A) You may turn in the direction of the arrow
B) You must stop
C) Pedestrian traffic only
D) You must go straight

6. When are you required to use your headlights during the day in Florida?
A) When it is raining
B) When driving through a tunnel
C) When driving on unlit roads
D) All of the above

7. What is the minimum penalty for a first DUI offense in Florida?
A) $250 fine
B) $500 fine
C) $1,000 fine
D) No fine, just a warning

8. What does a single solid yellow line in the center of the road indicate?
A) Passing allowed
B) No passing allowed
C) One-way street
D) Parking allowed

9. What is the speed limit near a school when children are present?
A) 15 mph
B) 20 mph
C) 25 mph
D) 30 mph

10. How should you behave when a school bus stops and its red lights are flashing?
A) Pass with caution
B) Stop within 10 feet of the bus
C) Stop completely, regardless of the direction you are traveling
D) Proceed only if you are on a one-way street

11. When are you required to use turn signals?
A) Only when turning left
B) Only when turning right
C) Every time you change lanes or turn
D) Only on the highway

12. What should you do if you see a stop sign with no stop line?
A) Come to a complete stop at the intersection
B) Stop only if there are other vehicles approaching
C) Proceed with caution
D) Stop at the edge of the road

13. What is the minimum distance allowed for parking near a fire hydrant?
A) 5 feet
B) 10 feet
C) 15 feet
D) 20 feet

14. Is it legal to pass on a two-lane road with double solid lines?
A) Yes, if there are no oncoming vehicles
B) No, it is always prohibited
C) Only at night
D) Only if the road is wide enough

15. When can you return to your lane after passing another vehicle?
A) When the vehicle you passed is no longer visible in your rearview mirror
B) Immediately after passing
C) When the vehicle you passed flashes its lights
D) When you are halfway down the road

16. What does a sign with a red circle and a white horizontal bar indicate?
A) No entry
B) Reserved parking
C) No left turn
D) Stop

17. If the road is icy, what is the recommended stopping distance compared to normal conditions?
A) The same
B) Double
C) Triple
D) Half

18. Which of the following actions is correct when approaching a roundabout?
A) Enter immediately
B) Yield to vehicles already in the roundabout
C) Always stop before entering
D) Enter only if no one is using the roundabout

19. What is the first thing you should do if your vehicle starts to skid?
A) Brake hard
B) Accelerate
C) Release the accelerator and steer into the skid
D) Turn the wheel in the opposite direction of the skid

20. What is the legal blood alcohol content (BAC) limit for drivers over 21 in Florida?
A) 0.05%
B) 0.08%
C) 0.10%
D) 0.02%

21. When must you turn on your vehicle's headlights and taillights?
A) One hour before sunset and one hour after sunrise
B) At sunset and sunrise
C) From half an hour after sunset until half an hour before sunrise
D) Only when it is dark

22. Is it legal to use a handheld cell phone while driving in Florida?
A) Yes, it is legal everywhere
B) No, it is illegal in all areas
C) Yes, except in school zones and construction zones
D) Only in rural areas

23. What is the minimum distance you must maintain from a cyclist when passing?
A) 1 foot
B) 2 feet
C) 3 feet
D) 5 feet

24. When are you required to stop for an approaching train?
A) When the lights are flashing
B) Only if the gates are down
C) When you hear the train
D) All of the above

25. What is the penalty for speeding in a school zone?
A) Double the fine
B) No fine
C) Regular fine
D) Increased points on your license without a fine

26. Which sign indicates that traffic is one-way?
A) Stop sign
B) "One Way" sign
C) Yield sign
D) Parking sign

27. When is it allowed to park in front of a private driveway?
A) Never
B) Only during the day
C) Only at night
D) If the driveway is yours

28. What is the penalty for disobeying a traffic officer's instructions?
A) Fine
B) Points on your license
C) Possible arrest
D) All of the above

29. When is it legal to pass a vehicle on the right?
A) When the vehicle ahead is turning left and there is enough space
B) Never
C) Only on highways
D) When the vehicle ahead is slow

30. If you see a flashing yellow arrow, what should you do?
A) Stop completely
B) Proceed with caution
C) Accelerate
D) Turn without stopping

31. Is wearing a seatbelt mandatory in Florida?
A) Only for front passengers
B) Yes, for all passengers
C) Only for the driver
D) No, it is not mandatory

32. What does a double solid yellow line in the center of the road indicate?
A) No passing allowed in either direction
B) Passing allowed in one direction only
C) One-way street
D) Passing allowed in both directions

33. When is it allowed to cross a solid yellow line?
A) To pass a slow-moving vehicle
B) Never
C) To turn left into a driveway or private road
D) To avoid an obstacle

34. In which situation must you always stop, regardless of signage?
A) When a school bus stops to load or unload children
B) When approaching an intersection without a traffic light
C) When there is heavy traffic
D) When a pedestrian is crossing the street

35. What should you do if your vehicle's wheels go off the road?
A) Get back on the road quickly
B) Stop immediately
C) Slow down gradually and re-enter the road cautiously
D) Accelerate to return to the road

36. What is the minimum distance for parking from an intersection?
A) 10 feet
B) 15 feet
C) 20 feet
D) 25 feet

37. What should you do if you see a flashing red light at an intersection?
A) Treat it like a green light
B) Come to a complete stop and proceed when safe
C) Accelerate
D) Treat it like a stop sign

38. When is it mandatory to use high beams?
A) On the highway
B) When there are no oncoming vehicles
C) In the city
D) During the day

39. In which circumstance is it allowed to make a U-turn?
A) Always
B) Never
C) Only on wide roads
D) Only if there are no signs prohibiting it and the road is clear

40. What is the maximum speed limit on an interstate highway in Florida?
A) 55 mph
B) 65 mph
C) 70 mph
D) 75 mph

41. If you approach a steady yellow traffic light, what should you do?
A) Speed up to cross the intersection
B) Stop if you can do so safely
C) Continue without stopping
D) Turn left

42. When can you continue driving if your vehicle's brakes fail?
A) Never
B) Only if you are close to home
C) Only on the highway
D) If you can use the handbrake

43. What is the first thing you should do in case of an accident?
A) Leave the scene
B) Check for injuries
C) Call the police
D) Exchange information with the other driver

44. What does a red arrow at an intersection indicate?
A) You must stop completely
B) You may turn cautiously
C) You must go straight
D) No left turn

45. When is it allowed to drive in a bus lane?
A) Never
B) Only at night
C) On weekends
D) Only if indicated by a sign

46. Which of the following actions should you avoid in case of hydroplaning?
A) Braking suddenly
B) Releasing the accelerator
C) Steering gently
D) Slowing down gradually

47. What is the maximum speed limit in a rural area in Florida?
A) 55 mph
B) 65 mph
C) 70 mph
D) 75 mph

48. How should you behave in heavy traffic?
A) Change lanes frequently to move faster
B) Stay in your lane and maintain a safe distance
C) Speed up to avoid getting stuck
D) Honk your horn to make space

49. What is the minimum recommended stopping distance from a red traffic light?
A) 5 feet
B) 10 feet
C) 15 feet
D) 20 feet

50. In which situation is it allowed to pass a vehicle in a passing zone?
A) When the vehicle is turning left
B) When the vehicle ahead is slow
C) Only during the day
D) Only if there is a dashed line

Answer Key

1B, 2B, 3B, 4B, 5A, 6D, 7C, 8B, 9B, 10C, 11C, 12A, 13C, 14B, 15A, 16A, 17C, 18B, 19C, 20B, 21C, 22C, 23C, 24D, 25A, 26B, 27A, 28D, 29A, 30B, 31B, 32A, 33C, 34A, 35C, 36C, 37B, 38B, 39D, 40C, 41B, 42A, 43B, 44A, 45A, 46A, 47C, 48B, 49D, 50A

Safe Driving Techniques and Driver Responsibility Quiz

1. What is the recommended following distance in normal driving conditions?
A) One second
B) Two seconds
C) Three seconds
D) Four seconds

2. When driving in adverse weather conditions, how should you adjust your following distance?
A) Maintain the same distance
B) Decrease the distance
C) Double the distance
D) Increase by one second

3. What is the first thing you should do before starting your vehicle?
A) Check your mirrors
B) Adjust your seatbelt
C) Adjust your seat and mirrors
D) Start the engine

4. When should you use your high beams?
A) In foggy conditions
B) When there are no oncoming vehicles
C) In urban areas
D) When following another vehicle closely

5. How should you react if you find yourself in a skid?
A) Brake hard
B) Accelerate
C) Steer in the direction of the skid
D) Steer in the opposite direction of the skid

6. What is the best way to handle a curve in the road?
A) Accelerate into the curve
B) Brake hard before the curve
C) Slow down before the curve, then accelerate gently through it
D) Maintain the same speed throughout the curve

7. What should you do if your vehicle begins to hydroplane?
A) Brake hard
B) Turn the steering wheel sharply
C) Ease off the accelerator and steer straight
D) Accelerate to regain traction

8. What is the most important factor in determining your safe speed in traffic?
A) The speed limit
B) The time of day
C) The road conditions and weather
D) The number of lanes

9. When is it necessary to yield the right-of-way to other vehicles?
A) When entering a roundabout
B) When making a right turn on red
C) When merging onto a highway
D) All of the above

10. How can you ensure that you are not in another driver's blind spot?
A) Drive at the same speed as the vehicle next to you
B) Stay directly behind the vehicle
C) Adjust your mirrors frequently
D) Avoid driving in the area beside the vehicle for long periods

11. What is the proper way to change lanes?
A) Signal, check mirrors, and change lanes quickly
B) Check mirrors, signal, and change lanes when safe
C) Signal, honk, and change lanes
D) Change lanes without signaling to avoid confusing other drivers

12. What should you do if an emergency vehicle is approaching with lights and sirens on?
A) Speed up to get out of the way
B) Pull over to the right and stop
C) Continue driving at the same speed
D) Move to the left lane

13. How often should you check your mirrors while driving?
A) Every 5 seconds
B) Every 10-15 seconds
C) Every 30 seconds
D) Only when changing lanes

14. When driving behind a large truck, how can you ensure the driver sees you?
A) Follow closely
B) Stay in the truck's blind spot
C) Position your vehicle so you can see the truck's mirrors
D) Flash your headlights

15. What should you do if you need to make an emergency stop?
A) Slam on the brakes
B) Pump the brakes repeatedly
C) Apply steady, firm pressure to the brake pedal
D) Pull the emergency brake

16. What is the most effective way to avoid collisions?
A) Drive faster than surrounding traffic
B) Use defensive driving techniques
C) Follow other vehicles closely
D) Ignore traffic signals

17. How should you handle driving in heavy traffic?
A) Weave in and out of lanes to find the fastest route
B) Drive closely to the car in front of you
C) Stay in your lane and maintain a safe following distance
D) Speed up to avoid congestion

18. What is the safest way to drive through an intersection?
A) Speed through to avoid getting stuck
B) Check all directions before entering the intersection
C) Follow the vehicle in front of you closely
D) Stop completely even if the light is green

19. What should you do if your brakes fail while driving?
A) Shift to a lower gear and use the parking brake
B) Accelerate to find a safe place to stop
C) Turn off the engine
D) Honk the horn to warn other drivers

20. When should you turn off your high beams?
A) When driving in rural areas
B) When you see an oncoming vehicle
C) When approaching a hill
D) When driving on a highway

21. How should you handle a tailgater?
A) Brake suddenly to warn them
B) Speed up to create distance
C) Move to another lane if possible and let them pass
D) Ignore them and continue driving

22. What is the first step you should take if your vehicle starts to overheat?
A) Turn off the air conditioning and turn on the heater
B) Continue driving to your destination
C) Stop immediately and add coolant
D) Increase your speed to cool the engine faster

23. What is the proper way to use anti-lock brakes (ABS) in an emergency?
A) Pump the brakes
B) Press the brake pedal firmly and hold it
C) Release the brake pedal intermittently
D) Apply the parking brake

24. How can you avoid being blinded by oncoming headlights at night?
A) Look directly into the headlights
B) Use your high beams
C) Look to the right edge of the road
D) Speed up to pass the vehicle

25. What should you do if you encounter an aggressive driver?
A) Engage with them and show your frustration
B) Slow down and let them pass
C) Speed up to get away from them
D) Block their path

26. How often should you check your tire pressure?
A) Once a year
B) Every time you change your oil
C) At least once a month
D) Only when you feel the tires are low

27. What should you do if you need to drive through deep water?
A) Drive quickly to avoid stalling
B) Test your brakes immediately after exiting the water
C) Avoid driving through deep water if possible
D) Drive in the center of the road

28. What is the correct response if you are involved in a minor accident with no injuries?
A) Leave the scene immediately
B) Exchange information with the other driver and report the accident if required
C) Call the police even if there are no injuries
D) Continue driving without stopping

29. How should you react to a tire blowout while driving?
A) Slam on the brakes
B) Grip the steering wheel firmly, steer straight, and gradually slow down
C) Turn the steering wheel sharply
D) Accelerate to regain control

30. What is the safest way to pass a motorcycle?
A) Pass closely to avoid oncoming traffic
B) Give the motorcycle a full lane width
C) Pass quickly to minimize the time next to the motorcycle
D) Honk to alert the motorcyclist

31. How should you drive in foggy conditions?
A) Use your high beams
B) Drive with your hazard lights on
C) Use low beams and reduce your speed
D) Follow the vehicle ahead closely

32. What is the appropriate action if your vehicle's engine stalls on the highway?
A) Stay in your lane and wait for help
B) Shift to neutral and restart the engine while moving
C) Steer to the side of the road and turn on your hazard lights
D) Exit the vehicle immediately

33. What should you do if you are driving and start feeling drowsy?
A) Turn up the radio
B) Open the windows for fresh air
C) Pull over to a safe place and rest
D) Continue driving to your destination

34. How can you reduce your risk of being in a collision when driving through an intersection?
A) Always speed through intersections
B) Avoid using turn signals
C) Cover the brake pedal and be prepared to stop
D) Ignore pedestrians

35. What is the best way to handle driving through a construction zone?
A) Speed up to pass through quickly
B) Slow down, obey all signs, and watch for workers
C) Ignore the speed limits
D) Weave through the barriers

36. How should you position your hands on the steering wheel for optimal control?
A) 10 and 2 o'clock
B) 8 and 4 o'clock
C) 9 and 3 o'clock
D) 12 and 6 o'clock

37. What is the correct procedure when approaching a stop sign?
A) Slow down and roll through the intersection if clear
B) Stop only if other vehicles are present
C) Come to a complete stop before the stop line or crosswalk
D) Stop only if a pedestrian is crossing

38. How should you handle driving on a slippery road?
A) Drive faster to get through quickly
B) Brake hard to maintain control
C) Reduce your speed and avoid sudden movements
D) Use cruise control

39. What should you do if you are driving and see an animal on the road?
A) Swerve to avoid it
B) Brake hard and stop
C) Slow down and try to pass around it
D) Honk the horn and speed up

40. When is it necessary to use a turn signal?
A) Only when turning left
B) Only when turning right
C) Every time you change lanes or make a turn
D) Only when merging onto a highway

41. What should you do if you are being tailgated?
A) Brake check the tailgater
B) Speed up to increase the distance
C) Move to another lane if possible and let them pass
D) Slow down abruptly to discourage them

42. What is the proper way to navigate a four-way stop?
A) The vehicle that arrives first has the right of way
B) The vehicle on the left has the right of way
C) Proceed without stopping if no other vehicles are present
D) Always yield to the vehicle on your right

43. How should you react to an emergency vehicle approaching from behind?
A) Speed up to get out of its way
B) Move to the right and stop
C) Continue driving at the same speed
D) Move to the left lane

44. What should you do if your car starts to fishtail?
A) Accelerate to regain control
B) Turn in the opposite direction of the fishtail
C) Steer into the direction of the fishtail
D) Brake hard

45. How can you prevent your car from skidding on a wet road?
A) Drive at the same speed as usual
B) Increase your speed
C) Slow down and avoid sudden turns
D) Use cruise control

46. What is the proper action to take if your vehicle begins to slide on ice?
A) Accelerate to regain control
B) Brake hard
C) Ease off the accelerator and steer gently
D) Turn sharply in the opposite direction

47. How should you drive through a roundabout?
A) Enter quickly to keep up with traffic
B) Yield to traffic already in the roundabout and enter when safe
C) Stop in the middle of the roundabout if unsure of your exit
D) Pass other vehicles in the roundabout

48. What is the most important factor in preventing a rollover accident?
A) Speeding through curves
B) Overloading the vehicle
C) Avoiding sharp turns at high speeds
D) Driving an SUV or truck

49. What should you do if your headlights suddenly go out while driving at night?
A) Brake hard and stop
B) Use your hazard lights and pull over
C) Speed up to reach your destination faster
D) Continue driving as usual

50. How often should you have your brakes checked by a professional?
A) Every 1,000 miles
B) Every 5,000 miles
C) Once a year
D) Every oil change

Answer Key

1C, 2C, 3C, 4B, 5C, 6C, 7C, 8C, 9D, 10D, 11B, 12B, 13B, 14C, 15C, 16B, 17C, 18B, 19A, 20B, 21C, 22A, 23B, 24C, 25B, 26C, 27C, 28B, 29B, 30B, 31C, 32C, 33C, 34C, 35B, 36C, 37C, 38C, 39C, 40C, 41C, 42A, 43B, 44C, 45C, 46C, 47B, 48C, 49B, 50D

EXAM SIMULATION

1. What is the legal blood alcohol content (BAC) limit for drivers over 21 in Florida?
A) 0.05%
B) 0.08%
C) 0.10%
D) 0.02%

2. When is it allowed to turn right at a red traffic light?
A) After making a complete stop and if there are no signs prohibiting it
B) Always
C) Never

3. How should you handle driving in foggy conditions?
A) Use high beams
B) Use low beams and reduce speed
C) Drive with hazard lights on

4. What should you do if your vehicle begins to skid?
A) Brake hard
B) Accelerate
C) Steer in the direction of the skid

5. What is the recommended following distance in normal driving conditions?
A) One second
B) Two seconds
C) Three seconds
D) Four seconds

6. How should you react if you find yourself in a skid?
A) Brake hard
B) Accelerate
C) Steer in the direction of the skid
D) Steer in the opposite direction of the skid

7. When must you yield the right-of-way to pedestrians?
A) Only at crosswalks
B) At all intersections, whether marked or unmarked
C) Only when traffic lights are red

8. What is the speed limit in a residential area in Florida?
A) 20 mph
B) 25 mph
C) 30 mph
D) 35 mph

9. When are you required to use your headlights during the day in Florida?
A) When it is raining
B) When driving through a tunnel
C) When driving on unlit roads
D) All of the above

10. What should you do if your brakes fail while driving?
A) Shift to a lower gear and use the parking brake
B) Accelerate to find a safe place to stop
C) Turn off the engine

11. When is it legal to pass another vehicle on the right?
A) When the vehicle ahead is turning left and there is enough space
B) Never
C) Only on highways
D) When the vehicle ahead is slow

12. How should you handle a tailgater?
A) Brake suddenly to warn them
B) Speed up to create distance
C) Move to another lane if possible and let them pass

13. What is the penalty for speeding in a school zone?
A) Double the fine
B) Regular fine
C) No fine

14. What is the proper way to change lanes?
A) Signal, check mirrors, and change lanes quickly
B) Check mirrors, signal, and change lanes when safe
C) Signal, honk, and change lanes
D) Change lanes without signalling

15. What should you do if you encounter an aggressive driver?

A) Engage with them
B) Speed up to get away
C) Slow down and let them pass
D) Block their path

16. How should you drive through a roundabout?

A) Enter quickly to keep up with traffic
B) Yield to traffic already in the roundabout and enter when safe
C) Stop in the middle of the roundabout if unsure of your exit

17. When should you use your high beams?

A) In foggy conditions
B) When there are no oncoming vehicles
C) In urban areas
D) When following another vehicle closely

18. How often should you check your tire pressure?

A) Once a year
B) Every time you change your oil
C) At least once a month

19. What is the correct action if your vehicle begins to hydroplane?

A) Brake hard
B) Ease off the accelerator and steer straight
C) Turn the steering wheel sharply
D) Accelerate to regain traction

20. What is the minimum following distance in adverse weather conditions?

A) Maintain the same distance
B) Decrease the distance
C) Double the distance
D) Increase by one second

21. What should you do if your vehicle's wheels go off the road?

A) Get back on the road quickly
B) Stop immediately
C) Slow down gradually and re-enter the road cautiously

22. How should you react to a tire blowout while driving?
A) Brake hard
B) Grip the steering wheel firmly, steer straight, and gradually slow down
C) Turn the steering wheel sharply
D) Accelerate to regain control

23. What is the maximum speed limit on an interstate highway in Florida?
A) 55 mph
B) 65 mph
C) 70 mph
D) 75 mph

24. How can you reduce your risk of being in a collision when driving through an intersection?
A) Always speed through intersections
B) Cover the brake pedal and be prepared to stop
C) Avoid using turn signals

25. What should you do if you are driving and see an animal on the road?
A) Swerve to avoid it
B) Slow down and try to pass around it
C) Honk the horn and speed up

26. How should you handle driving in heavy traffic?
A) Weave in and out of lanes to find the fastest route
B) Drive closely to the car in front of you
C) Stay in your lane and maintain a safe following distance
D) Speed up to avoid congestion

27. What is the correct response if you are involved in a minor accident with no injuries?
A) Leave the scene immediately
B) Exchange information with the other driver and report the accident if required
C) Call the police even if there are no injuries
D) Continue driving without stopping

28. When can you continue driving if your brakes fail?
A) Never
B) Only if you are close to home
C) Only on the highway
D) If you can use the handbrake

29. What is the most important factor in determining your safe speed in traffic?
A) The speed limit
B) The time of day
C) The road conditions and weather
D) The number of lanes

30. What should you do if your headlights suddenly go out while driving at night?
A) Brake hard and stop
B) Use your hazard lights and pull over
C) Speed up to reach your destination faster
D) Continue driving as usual

31. How should you handle driving on a slippery road?
A) Drive faster to get through quickly
B) Brake hard to maintain control
C) Reduce your speed and avoid sudden movements

32. What is the minimum distance allowed for parking near a fire hydrant?
A) 5 feet
B) 10 feet
C) 15 feet
D) 20 feet

33. What is the first thing you should do before starting your vehicle?
A) Check your mirrors
B) Adjust your seat and mirrors
C) Start the engine

34. What should you do if you start feeling drowsy while driving?
A) Turn up the radio
B) Open the windows for fresh air
C) Pull over to a safe place and rest

35. When is it necessary to use a turn signal?
A) Only when turning left
B) Only when turning right
C) Every time you change lanes or make a turn
D) Only when merging onto a highway

36. When is it allowed to pass a vehicle on the right?
A) When the vehicle is turning left and there is enough space
B) Never
C) Only on highways

37. How should you position your hands on the steering wheel for optimal control?
A) 10 and 2 o'clock
B) 8 and 4 o'clock
C) 9 and 3 o'clock
D) 12 and 6 o'clock

38. What should you do if an emergency vehicle is approaching with lights and sirens on?
A) Speed up to get out of the way
B) Pull over to the right and stop
C) Continue driving at the same speed
D) Move to the left lane

39. What is the correct action if you are being tailgated?
A) Brake check the tailgater
B) Speed up to increase the distance
C) Move to another lane if possible and let them pass

40. What is the minimum following distance you should maintain in normal driving conditions?
A) Two seconds
B) Three seconds
C) Four seconds

41. When should you turn off your high beams?
A) When driving in rural areas
B) When you see an oncoming vehicle
C) When approaching a hill
D) When driving on a highway

42. What is the proper way to navigate a four-way stop?
A) The vehicle that arrives first has the right of way
B) The vehicle on the left has the right of way
C) Proceed without stopping if no other vehicles are present

43. How often should you check your mirrors while driving?
A) Every 5 seconds
B) Every 10-15 seconds
C) Every 30 seconds
D) Only when changing lanes

44. What is the proper way to use anti-lock brakes (ABS) in an emergency?
A) Pump the brakes
B) Press the brake pedal firmly and hold it
C) Release the brake pedal intermittently
D) Apply the parking brake

45. How should you react if you encounter a flooded road?
A) Drive through it quickly
B) Avoid driving through deep water if possible
C) Drive slowly and test your brakes afterward

46. What is the proper response to a flashing yellow traffic light?
A) Stop completely
B) Proceed with caution
C) Speed up
D) Turn without stopping

47. What should you do if you are driving and your vehicle starts to fishtail?
A) Accelerate to regain control
B) Turn in the opposite direction of the fishtail
C) Steer into the direction of the fishtail
D) Brake hard

48. When should you use your low beams?
A) During heavy rain or fog
B) When driving at high speed
C) When driving in daylight
D) When driving on an empty highway

49. What is the best way to handle a curve in the road?
A) Accelerate into the curve
B) Slow down before the curve, then accelerate gently through it
C) Brake hard before the curve
D) Maintain the same speed throughout the curve

50. What is the appropriate action if your vehicle's engine stalls on the highway?

A) Stay in your lane and wait for help
B) Shift to neutral and restart the engine while moving
C) Steer to the side of the road and turn on your hazard lights
D) Exit the vehicle immediately

Answer Key

1B, 2A, 3B, 4C, 5C, 6C, 7B, 8B, 9D, 10A, 11A, 12C, 13A, 14B, 15C, 16B, 17B, 18C, 19B, 20C, 21C, 22B, 23C, 24B, 25B, 26C, 27B, 28A, 29C, 30B, 31C, 32C, 33B, 34C, 35C, 36A, 37C, 38B, 39C, 40B, 41B, 42A, 43B, 44B, 45B, 46B, 47C, 48A, 49B, 50C

EXAM SIMULATION 2

1. What should you do when approaching a railroad crossing with flashing lights?
A) Stop at least 15 feet from the tracks
B) Slow down and proceed with caution
C) Cross the tracks immediately
D) Continue driving at your current speed

2. How should you respond to a traffic light that has just turned yellow?
A) Speed up to cross the intersection before it turns red
B) Stop if you can do so safely
C) Proceed through the intersection
D) Turn left immediately

3. When is it acceptable to drive in a lane marked for buses only?
A) Never
B) During off-peak hours
C) If you are turning within the next block
D) On weekends

4. What is the safest way to merge onto a highway?
A) Stop at the end of the ramp and wait for a gap in traffic
B) Accelerate quickly and enter the first available gap
C) Match your speed to the traffic and merge when safe
D) Signal and slowly merge without adjusting your speed

5. When is it legal to drive with your parking lights on instead of headlights?
A) In heavy traffic
B) In foggy conditions
C) Only when parked
D) At dusk

6. How often should you have your vehicle's oil changed?
A) Every 1,000 miles
B) Every 3,000 to 5,000 miles
C) Every 10,000 miles
D) Once a year

7. What should you do if you see a pedestrian crossing the street at an unmarked crosswalk?
A) Slow down and proceed with caution
B) Stop and let the pedestrian cross
C) Honk your horn to alert the pedestrian
D) Speed up to pass before the pedestrian crosses

8. What is the purpose of a "No U-Turn" sign?
A) To prohibit U-turns in the specified area
B) To indicate a detour
C) To allow U-turns only for emergency vehicles
D) To guide traffic in the opposite direction

9. How should you handle a situation where another driver is following you too closely?
A) Brake sharply to warn them
B) Increase your speed to create more distance
C) Change lanes or pull over to let them pass
D) Flash your brake lights

10. What should you do if you see a school bus with flashing red lights on the opposite side of a divided highway?
A) Stop immediately
B) Continue driving cautiously
C) Proceed without stopping
D) Stop only if children are crossing

11. When can you legally use the shoulder of the road to pass another vehicle?
A) When the vehicle is turning left
B) When traffic is heavy
C) When the shoulder is wide enough
D) Never

12. What should you do if your vehicle starts to slide on ice?
A) Accelerate to regain control
B) Brake immediately
C) Ease off the accelerator and steer gently
D) Turn sharply in the opposite direction

13. What is the correct procedure for making a left turn at a green light without a green arrow?
A) Turn immediately without stopping
B) Wait for oncoming traffic to clear, then turn
C) Yield to oncoming traffic and pedestrians, then turn
D) Turn as soon as the light turns green

14. What does a solid white line on the right edge of the highway indicate?
A) A lane you can cross
B) A lane change area
C) The edge of the roadway
D) A passing zone

15. How should you handle driving through a work zone?
A) Speed up to pass through quickly
B) Obey all posted signs and flaggers
C) Follow the vehicle ahead closely
D) Ignore the speed limit

16. When is it necessary to use your turn signals?
A) Only when turning left
B) Only when changing lanes
C) Every time you turn or change lanes
D) Only when merging onto a highway

17. What should you do if you miss your exit on the highway?
A) Stop and back up
B) Take the next exit
C) Make a U-turn
D) Cross the median to get back to your exit

18. What is the correct way to use your headlights in the rain?
A) Use high beams to see better
B) Use low beams to avoid glare
C) Turn off headlights to avoid blinding other drivers
D) Use parking lights only

19. When is it legal to drive with a broken headlight?
A) Only during daylight hours
B) Only when the other headlight is working
C) Never
D) When driving on well-lit roads

20. What is the correct way to make a right turn at a red light in Florida?
A) Slow down and turn without stopping
B) Come to a complete stop and turn if no signs prohibit it
C) Turn immediately if there is no traffic
D) Turn only if there is a right turn lane

21. What should you do if you are involved in a collision with a parked vehicle?
A) Leave the scene
B) Leave a note with your contact information
C) Wait for the owner to return
D) Call the police and report the incident

22. What does a flashing red light at an intersection mean?
A) Proceed with caution
B) Yield to traffic
C) Stop and proceed when safe
D) Continue driving without stopping

23. How should you respond if you are driving and your vehicle starts to hydroplane?
A) Brake immediately
B) Steer sharply to regain control
C) Ease off the accelerator and steer straight
D) Accelerate to regain traction

24. What is the purpose of a "Merge" sign?
A) To warn drivers of merging traffic ahead
B) To indicate a lane closure
C) To direct traffic into a single lane
D) To signal the end of a divided highway

25. When should you use your hazard lights?
A) When driving in heavy traffic
B) When your vehicle is stopped or disabled on the road
C) When you are lost
D) When making a sharp turn

26. How should you handle a situation where a large truck is turning right?
A) Speed up to pass the truck
B) Stay close behind the truck
C) Wait for the truck to complete its turn before proceeding
D) Move to the left lane to pass the truck

27. What is the correct response if you are driving and an animal suddenly appears in front of your vehicle?
A) Swerve to avoid the animal
B) Brake firmly and try to stop
C) Speed up to avoid hitting the animal
D) Honk your horn and continue driving

28. When should you check your blind spots?
A) Before changing lanes or merging
B) Only when parking
C) When driving in heavy traffic
D) When making a left turn

29. What should you do if you see a vehicle coming toward you in your lane?
A) Speed up to avoid the vehicle
B) Swerve to the left
C) Brake and move to the right
D) Honk your horn and flash your lights

30. What is the purpose of a "Yield" sign?
A) To instruct drivers to give the right of way to other vehicles
B) To indicate a stop is required
C) To direct traffic to merge
D) To signal a one-way street

31. What is the minimum distance you should maintain from a fire hydrant when parking?
A) 5 feet
B) 10 feet
C) 15 feet
D) 20 feet

32. How should you handle driving in a construction zone?
A) Speed up to avoid delays
B) Follow posted signs and flagger instructions
C) Weave through traffic cones
D) Ignore the speed limit

33. What should you do if your car stalls while driving?
A) Stay in your lane and wait for help
B) Try to restart the engine while driving
C) Steer to the side of the road and turn on hazard lights
D) Exit the vehicle immediately

34. When should you increase your following distance?
A) When driving in heavy traffic
B) When driving in ideal weather conditions
C) When following a motorcycle
D) When following a large truck or bus

35. What is the correct way to use anti-lock brakes (ABS) in an emergency situation?
A) Pump the brakes
B) Press the brake pedal firmly and hold it
C) Release the brake pedal intermittently
D) Apply the parking brake

36. How should you position your side mirrors to reduce blind spots?
A) So you can see the sides of your car
B) So you can see the road directly behind you
C) So you can see the lanes next to you
D) So you can see the horizon

37. What should you do if your car starts to overheat?
A) Turn off the air conditioning and turn on the heater
B) Pull over and turn off the engine
C) Increase your speed to cool the engine
D) Turn off the heater and continue driving

38. What is the correct response to a flashing yellow arrow in a turn lane?
A) Turn immediately
B) Stop completely
C) Proceed with caution and yield to oncoming traffic
D) Ignore it and wait for a green arrow

39. How should you handle a situation where another driver is tailgating you?
A) Brake suddenly to warn them
B) Speed up to create more distance
C) Move to another lane if possible and let them pass
D) Flash your brake lights

40. When is it legal to use a handheld cell phone while driving in Florida?
A) Never
B) Only in rural areas
C) Only when stopped at a red light
D) Only in emergencies

41. What is the proper way to merge onto a busy highway?
A) Stop at the end of the ramp until you can merge
B) Match your speed to the traffic and merge when safe
C) Slow down and wait for a gap
D) Accelerate quickly and force your way into traffic

42. What should you do if you are driving and feel drowsy?
A) Turn up the radio
B) Open the windows for fresh air
C) Pull over and rest
D) Continue driving to your destination

43. How should you react to a stop sign with no stop line or crosswalk?
A) Slow down and roll through the intersection
B) Stop completely before entering the intersection
C) Proceed without stopping if no other vehicles are present
D) Stop only if there is traffic

44. What is the purpose of a "Do Not Enter" sign?
A) To indicate a restricted area
B) To indicate a one-way street
C) To indicate an entrance to a private property
D) To warn drivers not to enter a particular roadway

45. What should you do if you see a vehicle approaching in your lane?
A) Speed up to avoid the vehicle
B) Swerve to the left
C) Brake and move to the right
D) Honk your horn and continue driving

46. What should you do if your car stalls while driving?
A) Stay in your lane and wait for help
B) Try to restart the engine while driving
C) Steer to the side of the road and turn on hazard lights
D) Exit the vehicle immediately

47. How should you handle a curve on a wet road?
A) Brake hard before the curve
B) Accelerate through the curve
C) Slow down before the curve
D) Maintain your speed through the curve

48. What should you do if you see an emergency vehicle with flashing lights on the side of the road?
A) Speed up to pass the vehicle
B) Change lanes away from the emergency vehicle if possible
C) Stop immediately
D) Continue driving at the same speed

49. What should you do if your car begins to fishtail?
A) Brake hard
B) Steer in the direction of the fishtail
C) Accelerate to regain control
D) Turn the wheel in the opposite direction of the fishtail

50. What should you do if your vehicle's tires go off the pavement?
A) Swerve back onto the road immediately
B) Brake hard and stop
C) Slow down gradually and steer back onto the road
D) Accelerate to regain control

Answer Key

1A, 2B, 3C, 4C, 5C, 6B, 7B, 8A, 9C, 10B, 11D, 12C, 13C, 14C, 15B, 16C, 17B, 18B, 19C, 20B, 21B, 22C, 23C, 24A, 25B, 26C, 27B, 28A, 29C, 30A, 31C, 32B, 33C, 34D, 35B, 36C, 37B, 38C, 39C, 40D, 41B, 42C, 43B, 44D, 45C, 46C, 47C, 48B, 49B, 50C

ONLINE QUIZ SIMULATOR

We are excited to present you with an exclusive additional resource included with your purchase of the book "Florida DMV Exam Prep": our Online Quiz Simulator. This innovative tool is designed to provide you with a more comprehensive and interactive study experience, helping you prepare effectively for the DMV exam.

What Does the Online Simulator Offer?

- **Interactive Quizzes:** Access a wide range of quizzes covering all areas of the DMV exam, including road signs, traffic laws, and safe driving practices. Each quiz is structured to reflect the official exam format, allowing you to familiarize yourself with the types of questions you'll encounter.

- **Instant Feedback:** Receive immediate feedback on each question, with detailed explanations to help you understand why an answer is correct or incorrect. This enables you to learn more effectively and consolidate your knowledge.

- **Exam Simulations:** Try full exam simulations to assess your level of preparation. These simulations are timed and structured exactly like the DMV exam, helping you better manage your time and reduce exam anxiety.

- **Unlimited Access:** Study as much and as often as you want, without limits. You can access the online simulator from your computer, tablet, or smartphone, making it easy to integrate into your daily routine.

How to Access the Online Simulator?

Step 1: Open the camera app on your smartphone or use a QR code reader app.
Step 2: Point the camera at the QR code.
Step 3: Click on the link that appears to access the digital color version of the book.

Made in United States
Orlando, FL
18 December 2024